ANDY MATTHEWS
GREATEST HAUNTS

D1347773

ANDY MATTHEWS
GREATEST HAUNTS

Don't believe in ghosts? Read the stories
of the ghosts we recorded!

As seen on BBC

foulsham
LONDON • NEW YORK • TORONTO • SYDNEY

foulsham

The Oriel, Thames Valley Court, 183–187 Bath Road, Slough, Berkshire, SL1 4AA, England

Foulsham books can be found in all good bookshops and direct from www.foulsham.com

ISBN: 978-0-572-03543-3

Printed in Great Britain by Thomson Litho, East Kilbride

Dedication

For my wife Stacey, my three boys and my mum and dad, all of whom have for ever been at my side.

Tread softly, for you may hear me weep
Night has gone, but daylight brings no sleep
Arrested in my prime, my soul kept at bay
My feelings within remain to stay.
Forever locked in a timeless state
The world I knew, ignorant of my fate.
Hidden in the shadows it knows not me
Until death becomes life, and I am set free.

Andy Matthews, 2009

Acknowledgements

Special thanks to Coco Television, Jane Wardrop, Mark Cowden, Graham Matthews, David Starkey and my Nan.

Photo of Bowden House courtesy of Richard Knight.

Photo of the Tower of London courtesy of Viki Male.

Contents

A Question of Life after Death?

Picture yourself for a moment at the point of death as you prepare to embark upon that final departure across heaven and earth, with only your own ideals and beliefs to guide you. Stepping uncertainly into the beyond, unknowing and fearing to tread, you spy a light, and the realisation dawns that you are faced with a decision. Do you go forward into the unknown, or resist whatever awaits you and decide to stay within surroundings that you recognise and trust?

Are all of us so willing to move on when time beckons us? Certainly for those who submit to the natural order of life, the answer to the ultimate question will finally be recognised. But what of those who remain behind, desperately clinging on to a life that is no longer there to live? Lost and confused, perhaps they wander aimlessly, searching for some scrap of physical identity with little or no comprehension that they are indeed trapped only by their stubborn refusal to release themselves from their own mortality.

I have never been fond of the word 'ghost', for to be a ghost one would have to be non-existent, and in a realistic universe that simply isn't possible. It is a scientific fact that matter has energy. As a life form made up of vibrating energy particles, is it therefore so ridiculous to imagine that life continues to exist after our bodily death, albeit without the clanking chains and chilly fingers so often remarked upon in ghost stories?

The natural world we live in is governed by the rules of nature; its intricate balance and unending cycle of birth, life, death and rebirth are apparent in all living things that populate our planet. As the energy we call life is engulfed and reborn over and over, life does indeed find a way to survive, driven by forces that make up the mysterious matrix of our energy-driven universe.

We call unexplained events 'paranormal', but perhaps 'hidden' or 'natural' would be more appropriate, for surely it is plausible to suggest that humans have overcomplicated the concepts of life after death simply because our experience does not fit the laws of physics.

Any scientist or philosopher will tell you that the world around us supposedly has 11 other dimensions that our human brains for some reason refuse to let us see. But just because we can't see something with the naked eye doesn't necessarily mean that it isn't there. Proof of the existence of an afterlife and the largely incomprehensible theories of why some of us remain on the earthly plane in an energy-based, non-physical state are – let's face it – impossible to prove. However, on a personal level, such concepts are widely accepted by individuals across all countries, cultures and belief systems.

The theory of spiritual survival intrigued me so much that I began to research the subject in great detail, and in my attempt to find some answers spent two years training as a medium. Over the years, I have stumbled across some fascinating and sometimes frightening examples of paranormal activity that although very extraordinary, offered nothing in the way of scientific proof. However, in my experience the truth certainly is in the eye of the beholder. It just depends on whether or not we dare to look.

This book features a selection of case studies from the UK and Ireland that I have compiled from over 12 years investigating the paranormal. Many of the accounts occurred during the filming of various TV series I have worked on over the years including Lion Television's *Ghost Detectives*, *Ghost Watch from the Tower of London* and BBC1's *Northern Ireland's Greatest Haunts*.

I won't promise you answers; but as you read this book, pondering on the theories of life after death, try to keep an open mind with this thought in your head: what if our lives are merely stepping-stones on a long and winding road called existence, and what would happen if occasionally we lose our way?

Note. Some of the words and phrases you come across in this book might be unfamiliar if you are new to the world of the paranormal. You will find clarification and explanation in the final chapter, 'So You Want to Hunt Ghosts'.

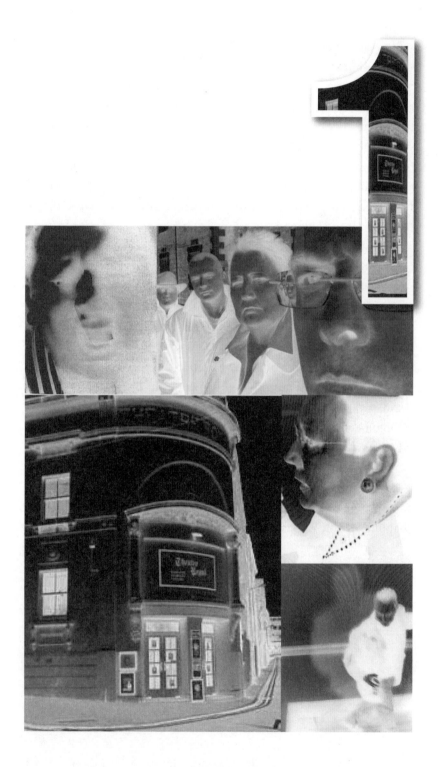

The Witch, the Ouija Board and the Fear Factor

I remember the moment. I remember where I was and how confused I felt when the thought first struck me to write a book. In the words of John Lennon, it felt more like a happening than an idea, and as I stood on Margate's solitary beach taking in the early-morning sea air, I found myself once again contemplating the logic of what I had witnessed the night before.

Gazing out to sea, the realisation dawned on me that perhaps our cosy little world has more hidden secrets that any of us could ever possibly imagine. Flashbacks of the previous night's events came to me once again, but I took some comfort from the notion that it is perfectly acceptable to fear what one does not understand.

The séance had gone horribly wrong and I recalled the panic that swept through the investigation team as the lone entity we were trying to help ran amok, before finally realising that its only course of escape was to hide in one of us. My heart raced as I watched it apparently jump from one person to another before retreating back up into the fly tower of the theatre, perhaps the only sanctuary it had known for over 300 years.

What I had witnessed had certainly changed my perception of ghosts. Furthermore, in the cold light of day, I found myself questioning everything I had been taught as a child and been brought up to believe.

The ocean before me was vast and for the first time I witnessed the tides of the sea from a different perspective. The true wonderment of the natural world, its laws, its superb intricate balance and its complex unending cycle of birth, life, death and rebirth in all living things made me feel very small and insignificant, yet at the same time essential to the mechanics of the universe.

I now possessed a new chapter of knowledge that had evaded me for so long, an understanding of life that in the cold light of day still prevailed within me. There never was any mystery because the answers had been there all the time; I had just never bothered to open my eyes and look. The waves crashed before me with thunderous applause, and as I stepped back to avoid the incoming wash, I wondered whether Mother Nature had just acknowledged my reasoning.

The witch

My childhood holds very dear memories and I consider myself extremely lucky to have been born to two of the most wonderful people to have walked the earth, my Mum and Dad. The youngest of three brothers, I was always the loveable rogue of the litter, getting away with everything and generally rebelling against authority. But through all of these growing pains and learning curves, my parents were always there for me, never failing to do what they did best, and for this reason I always felt protected and loved from a very early age. There was, however, one occasion when I had to stand my own ground completely alone.

I was six years old when I first saw the witch. I can vividly remember lying in bed and hearing the dreadful sounds that signalled her approach. The booming, crashing footsteps ascending the stairs at a speed no human could produce, the shuffling, the cackling. All these sounds became so familiar to me that I eventually gave them a name: Witchypoo night.

I was always paralysed; I couldn't sit up, call out or move in any direction. The witch would come crashing into my room casting obscene shadows on the bedroom wall and through the gloom of the darkened room I watched, terrified, as she shuffled over to the left-hand side of the bed. Then, with her withered old face almost touching mine, she would start to tickle me.

I couldn't cry, laugh or even attempt scratching to relieve the tickling sensations I had to endure. Even the simplest task of moving my head to avoid her warty, toothless, grinning face was impossible. All I could do was close my eyes and wait for the tickling to cease, for once I could feel it no more I knew she would be gone. Afterwards I would lie there in the dim light not daring to move, my eyes searching each corner of the room for any sign of the old crone with long straw-like hair and wearing putrid rags. I never thought of her as a ghost. To me she was a wicked witch who, as I reached the age of seven or eight, became not so much an object of fear but more of an annoyance. I began to get angry at her persistence and in my head would shout at her to go away. As my fear receded, I made it quite clear in my subconscious that she was not welcome back.

Eventually her visits lessened and on the occasions she did appear I would not allow her near the bed. It was like a battle of wills that surprisingly I found I could win. Towards the end of these childhood experiences, I was amused to find that the scary old hag was reduced to shuffling around the room unable to come near me or the bed, until one night she vanished and never returned.

I kept these incidents to myself, although my dear mum does vaguely recall me telling her of a witch that used to tickle me, but I made no great fuss of the apparent visitations. Looking back now, I tend to regard what happened to me as a form of sleep paralysis in which although the body is asleep, the brain subconsciously remains awake. When we sleep, our bodies go into a form of natural paralysis to avoid us acting out our dreams. But before I fully disregard the witch as nothing more than a nightmare, it is relevant to note that many people worldwide have reported similar experiences involving an old crone-like witch pinning them to their beds.

Could the hag therefore be some wandering, annoying entity or a simple fragment of human imagination? Films like *The Wizard of Oz* and, my favourite as a child, *Pufnstuf*, starring Jack Wild, both featured a wicked witch, and although fun to watch they could certainly have triggered nightmarish images in a young, impressionable mind.

The memory of those Witchypoo nights stayed with me through to adulthood, fuelling an interest in ghost theory that would eventually lead me to study parapsychology. So in retrospect, the experience remains a favourable episode from my past.

The Ouija board

'My house is haunted,' stated my best mate while we were out on a bike ride one summer's day in 1979. There were five of us, all aged between 14 and 16, and we all reacted as kids of that age would: we laughed and generally took the mick until Ray began to tell his story in more detail.

He and his younger brother shared a bedroom in a modest, three-bedroom, terraced council house. For the past few nights, whilst they lay in their beds, the temperature in the room would inexplicably drop and both felt they were being watched. On some occasions the bedroom door would slowly creak open of its own accord and then violently slam shut, leaving them both terrified. His mother also claimed to have seen the ghost of a man wandering around the upstairs landing late at night.

Eventually the apparent ghostly phenomena took its toll on the family and they persuaded the council to allow them to move to a house further up the street. The day after they moved out, the house was empty but Ray still had a front door key. If we were going to investigate and look for the ghost, then now would be our only opportunity. Patiently, we waited for nightfall.

We entered the house giggling and made silly *whoo-whoo* noises as we crept up the darkened staircase by torchlight. Upon reaching the landing by Ray's old bedroom door we stopped, all feeling a high degree of trepidation that began to escalate at an alarming rate. Nobody wanted to admit to being scared, so despite the agitation, we forced ourselves ahead into the empty bedroom, and for a moment felt comforted by the light from the streetlamp outside illuminating us through the window.

Feeling more relaxed now, we made ourselves comfortable on the floor and lit up some cigarettes. Everything was calm until Chris, the eldest of our gang, revealed that he had a Ouija board in his bag. He set it up on the floor, placing a small glass in the centre; the excitement was intense. We all placed one finger on the glass and asked in a not-too-serious way if there was anybody there. Nothing happened – and even if it had, we had no idea how to read or use the thing anyway. What happened next, though, I now tend to regard as one of those learning curves my dad used to tell me about.

The banging started: booming, crashing noises so loud it sounded as though the house was under demolition. Through all of this sudden mayhem, we barely seemed to notice the sharp temperature reduction or the shadow that appeared lurking in the open doorway. All of this happened so fast that our attention had been drawn away from the glass, which was weaving its way around the board in all directions at great speed.

Of course, that was enough for us! We ran out of there as fast as we could, never stopping until we were halfway down the road. My first brush with an apparent haunting had resulted in a mad rush to the door. So ended my first lesson, for I now possessed a high degree of respect for the unknown, and to this day, apart from observing the process under controlled conditions, I have never touched a Ouija board since.

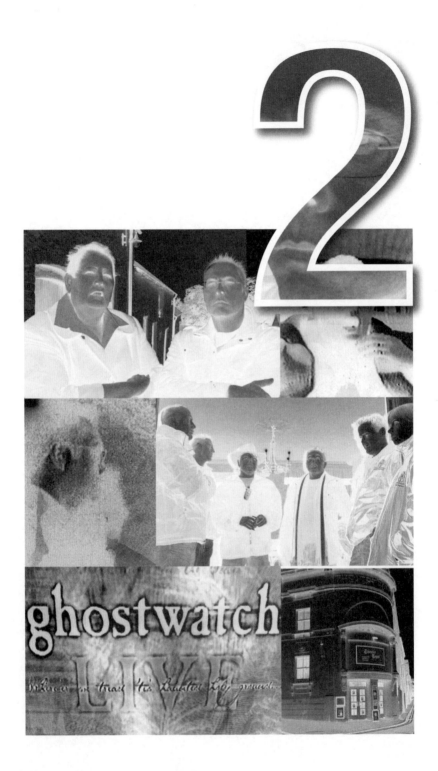

The Ghosts of Sowerby – Part 1

As the famous Vulcan character from the classic sci-fi TV series *Star Trek* once said, 'For everything there is a first time,' and Mr Spock was right. Ghost hunting, paranormal investigations, psychic study, whatever your preference may be for the title of this unusual pastime, finding yourself walking into an allegedly haunted building for the first time to look for evidence of a haunting conjures up a mixture of excitement and dread.

The paranormal had always been a hobby of mine, yet following a number of unnerving experiences in my 20s, my enthusiasm with ghosts had diminished, leaving me with an ignorant denial of all things supernatural. I now know the reasons why I had those particular experiences, but back then it took a lot of soul-searching and guidance from a very special medium in order for me to face those events again.

The year was 1999. I was a ghost hunter and I was back, full of courage and ready to meet the challenge of understanding, rather than fearing, whatever hides away in the shadows of our mind's eye.

The Haunting of the Sowerby Arms

The Sowerby Arms is a typical English rural pub. Old-fashioned and antiquated in its design, it remains virtually untouched by modern times. Central to a small village in Bedfordshire, the pub was supposedly the last stopping point for the condemned as they were marched through the village to the gallows in times gone by, to face their summary execution, courtesy of the hangman's noose.

Local tales of the ghostly manifestation of a shepherd seen on a number of occasions by employees and customers alike are what first brought the case to our attention.

Eyewitnesses say that the figure once appeared to a hardy builder, who at the time was under contract to renovate the restaurant. He had scoffed at the ghost stories served to him by the locals, until one day he himself came face to face with the wandering shepherd. Disorientated and gripped with fear, the ashen-faced builder left his tools behind at the pub that very day and never returned.

As a child, the landlady's son often complained that there were people in his bedroom keeping him awake at night. This could be construed as the fanciful imagination of a child, but the boy described these visitors in great detail. They were allegedly smaller than the average man and were wearing scruffy, putrid, old-fashioned clothes. When asked by his mother if they had ever spoken to him, the little boy would collapse into fits of giggles. 'Yes, Mummy, but they talk funny. It makes me laugh.' Perhaps the boy was referring to some old form of spoken English.

The theory certainly makes sense. If you imagine yourself to be a 17th-century servant, lost between worlds and perhaps unaware that you are, in fact, dead, then logically to communicate successfully, you will utilise the only language known to you. A more plausible possibility is that the entire episode could have been nothing more than the product of a child's imaginative mind, creating false reality whilst attempting to make logical sense of a recurring dream. You never know with children, but I think that once having read this chapter you will agree that this incident was by no means an early version of the *Teletubbies*.

Haunted?

Lovely spooky stories, yes. But did these reports really warrant a full-scale investigation? The answer to this question was decided by one telephone call to Sheila, the landlady of the pub. She informed me that for many years she had received numerous complaints from her customers of being poked or pushed in the public bar by a seemingly unseen assailant. As if this wasn't enough, the recently renovated restaurant area had suddenly attained an unwelcome presence and when left alone in this area, employees reported experiencing feelings of extreme anxiety causing some simply to refuse to enter alone.

Christmas in the pub seemed to be an unfavourable time of year with the ghosts, for once the decorations were hung, the staff would find them next morning pulled down and torn to shreds. Sheila added that one year, paper streamers had literally disappeared from the ceiling without trace, never to be seen again. I asked her if this occurrence was localised to one particular area of the building, to which she replied, 'Yes, the restaurant.'

It was late November 1999 and with Christmas only weeks away, this did appear to be an opportune time to tempt a poltergeist out to play. The investigation team assembled consisted of Ross Hemsworth and my brother Graham Matthews, both founders of the Phantom or Fraud Project (a team who would later become TV's *Ghost Detectives*) and researcher Suzie Miller. For this case we also felt it necessary to bring in Marion Goodfellow, our new medium, and David O'Neil, a friend of mine, who had kindly volunteered at short notice to assist with the rigging of cameras and monitoring equipment.

I introduced myself to Sheila and thanked her on behalf of the team for allowing us to invade her pub for a period of four nights. She indicated that the areas of reported activity were not confined to the restaurant and public bar, but also included the renovated attic, stairs, kitchen and three guest bedrooms. Unfortunately, all

Andy gathers the investigating team

three bedrooms were occupied and therefore out of bounds to us. This was indeed a shame, as Sheila went on to tell me that some guests had on occasions been disturbed in the night and checked out the very next morning, cancelling their booking. Some would leave rather hurriedly saying nothing, whilst others would enquire as to whether the pub had a ghost! On one occasion, a guest had awoken feeling as though he was being strangled in his bed!

With the rigging almost completed, I decided to have a chat with some of the locals in the public bar. They all had a story to tell, and eventually suspicions as to who was haunting the pub developed into a light-hearted argument. But these conversations confirmed to me that everything Sheila had told me was indeed accurate.

Up in the attic, despite trying a variety of connection leads, the CCTV cameras refused to work properly, although mysteriously everything functioned perfectly in the corridor outside. Furthermore, two sets of new rechargeable batteries for our digital camera inexplicably drained of all power the moment we entered through the diminutive doorway. It is easy to assume that paranormal activity is the cause of equipment failure in these situations, but despite an unwelcome feeling emanating from the attic, I refused to let my imagination get the better of me.

On my return to the bar, I discovered that Marion had arrived, bringing with her a personality that lit up the tiny bar like a Christmas tree. We had some time to spare, so following a brief introduction she agreed to give my sceptical friend David his first psychic reading. I joined them at the table and answered David's look of amusement with raised eyebrows.

'I have your grandfather here and he wishes to talk to you,' said Marion. David sat back crossing his arms.

'I never knew my grandfather,' he replied smartly.

'He knows you,' answered Marion. She went on to state that the only picture David owned of his grandfather was of him astride a horse, dressed in military uniform. Upon hearing this David went very pale and confirmed that this was a fact that only he could possibly know to be true.

Marion continued. She began to divulge dates, names and information, such as where his family originated, the name of the town they lived in, his father's occupation, his mother's blindness in one eye, and even David's subsequent redundancy that has left him, in the words of his grandfather, watching time tick away. With tears welling in his eyes, David confirmed that he does tend to sit at home with time on his hands, gazing at the clock. Even more sensational, he explained that the clock in question was a family heirloom, originally owned by his grandfather.

This was the first time that I had seen Marion deliver a psychic reading to an independent stranger other than myself and score an incredible 10 out of 10. Could it be possible that Marion was reading thoughts telepathically from David's mind, rather than communicating with a lost loved one? Once you have ruled out luck and coincidence, you are still left with two theories, both as fantastical as the other and equally unexplainable. Needless to say, David was at a loss for words.

Marion making contact in the restaurant

Me, a medium?

The evening was wearing on and I still hadn't had the chance to have a good look around the building. So leaving David to his thoughts, Marion and I made our way through to the restaurant area. We stood in the doorway like a couple of gunfighters surveying a Wild West saloon, only this saloon was empty – or so it appeared.

'What do you feel?' asked Marion, softly.

'Nothing,' I replied.

'Look beyond your senses,' she whispered. 'You feel anticipation. Don't hide from it, open up to it and look again, not with your eyes but with your own psyche.'

As I surveyed the restaurant for the second time, I found myself experiencing an unusual, instinctive attraction to certain areas of the room, an attraction that seemed to intensify with each passing second. The urge to walk forward and explore these areas was overwhelming, magnetic even, but I resisted momentarily, collecting my thoughts.

At our first meeting, Marion had indicated to me that I possessed a strong psychic vibration that with a little training could eventually open up a career for me as a working clairvoyant. Although I had always had my suspicions of this psychic ability, my own basic instincts of fear and uncertainty had always prevented me from taking that first step forward – until now.

I had heard mediums say that to open up requires no physical effort; you simply open your spiritual psyche, embrace your thoughts and trust that your spirit guide will protect you. I had always felt that my guide or protector was my grandmother. She died in 1948 and so I never knew her in life, but I always had a strong indication that she was always there for me in times of need.

With her presence foremost in my thoughts, I opened my psyche and took my first steps forward into the restaurant, whilst making sure that Marion and my common sense were not far behind me. Beautifully laid out, cosy and romantic, the restaurant was a touch more modern than the rest of the building. The entire area was on level ground and contained two dining areas set between a walkway, with a small bar tucked away in the right-hand corner. I made my way down the aisle to the far left-hand corner of the restaurant and suddenly connected with what I can only describe as a blanket of freezing cold energy.

I was amazed; I could actually feel the texture. It had the softness of velvet and the tingling of static.

'There's something here,' I murmured, a little nervously.

'I know,' replied Marion. 'Now move your hand slowly up and then down.' I followed her instructions and discovered that the energy dominated an area almost a metre deep and anywhere above or below this level felt completely normal.

Digesting this somewhat weird experience, I now noticed that other areas of the restaurant began to beckon. Marion instructed me to move around the entire restaurant and to call out if I felt any further changes in the atmosphere. Curiously, I continued, thankful that no customers were present to raise an amused eyebrow. There appeared to be two main lines of energy horizontally crossing with each other. Following my instincts, I traced the focal point to the aisle separating the two dining areas.

I was unaware that during my walkabout, David and Sheila had joined Marion and been observing my actions. Marion congratulated me and then to my surprise informed me that she had already toured the restaurant on her arrival and had found exactly the same points of energy as I had in exactly the same places. Furthermore, David had been a witness to this and verbally confirmed that Marion had indeed already found these areas while I was upstairs in the attic.

The word 'coincidence' sprang to mind and then just as quickly sprang out again. Sheila requested that I show her exactly where these energy lines apparently crossed. I made my way back down the aisle and once having located the area for the second time, I turned and indicated the location to her, and she stared back at me in disbelief.

Her next sentence was spoken rather shakily: 'That's it! That's where she's been seen, right on that spot!' she exclaimed.

'Who?' I asked.

'A woman, dressed in white,' she whispered, 'and this is also the exact area where we find the torn up decorations at Christmas!'

David's jaw dropped, and both Sheila and I looked to Marion for an explanation.

'Don't you see?' she began. 'It's an energy line. Spirits no longer have bodies made up of flesh and blood; all that remains of them is pure energy. They use these energy lines as a means to travel from A to B.'

As a novice and ever ready to question, I enquired that if this was indeed the case, then why don't the spirits move on. Why do they stay here if they are capable of travelling further afield? I listened as Marion gave her opinion that perhaps they are trapped here, maybe held in by forces of nature that we don't understand. Perhaps they consider this pub to be their home, in which case why should they wish to leave?

As I pondered all these possibilities, my mind searched frantically for some rational solution to explain the previous five minutes of my life. Had I really made contact with the remnants of a ghost's energy field or was I becoming over-keen to believe in a draughty old pub? Furthermore, did any of us have the right to interfere with things we knew so very little about? In desperate need of a cigarette, I made my way outside.

The attic

The decision was made later in the evening that a séance would take place, not in the restaurant as expected, but in the attic. The team would always leave Marion to decide where a séance would take place and, on this occasion, it was Marion's opinion that the attic would be the ideal place to begin. At a little after 11pm, just around closing time, we made our way upstairs to the very top of the building, leaving two team members in the control room to monitor the rest of the rooms.

The attic itself had been converted into a quaint little sitting room and boasted all the comforts of any ordinary household lounge. Marion quickly made herself comfortable in the main chair, leaving me to take my place on the three-piece suite, together with my brother Graham, who would film the entire séance with a hand-held, battery-operated video camera. Lastly, our researcher Suzie

Andy and Marion, long-time collaborators

took up her position by the door and settled herself down to take notes of whatever happened.

Regardless of our beliefs, Marion began by instructing all present to form a protective psychic shield around ourselves. According to mediums, this action is essential for all sensitives in order to block any unwanted contact. If during the séance Marion came into contact with a disruptive or negative entity, then her guide would immediately force this entity to leave. The danger then is that the spirit may attempt to re-establish contact with another clairvoyant, one who is weaker and less experienced. It made no difference to me as to whether the psychic barrier was real or imaginary; all I know is that once I had put it there I felt safe and secure.

My role that night was to assist Marion as she slipped into a form of self-hypnotic trance. Once this state had been achieved, then effectively a line of contact would exist, enabling spiritual entities to manifest themselves through her. Counting Marion down from 20, it wasn't long before she appeared to have achieved the correct state of consciousness required for the séance to commence.

Three minutes passed by in complete silence, save for the gentle sound of the tape in the video recorder as it revolved round and around the spools, recording nothing more than Marion apparently snoozing in the chair.

Suddenly the shrill call of a fox cut through the silent night air, causing everybody to jump several feet to the left. Marion, on the other hand, had not moved a muscle. She remained motionless, her face a peaceful blanket of non-expression. I leaned forward, indicating to the rest of the team that I was ready to commence stage two of the séance. The time for contact had arrived. 'Is there anybody here who would like to talk to us?' I asked.

Frowning, Marion erupted into a loud, vigorous coughing fit that continued unabated for around 15 to 20 seconds until finally she slumped back into the chair displaying all the attributes of an extremely ill old man.

'Who are you?' I continued. The response was preceded by more coughing, followed by a bout of laboured breathing that accompanied every word uttered by this apparent spirit.

'I am Tom.' The hairs on the back of my neck stood on end and having glanced behind me to ensure that there was no open window to account for this, I continued a little tentatively, searching for any indication of faking from Marion.

'Hello, Tom. Can you tell me why you are here in this place?' I asked.

'I live here,' came the reply.

'Tom, are you aware that there are other people living in this place too?'

The quick response was tinged with anger: 'Trespassers, always in my way!'

He was showing signs of agitation and proceeded to cough even more violently, whilst clutching his chest as if in great pain. I delayed any further questioning until Tom had settled down.

'Tom, you say you live here. Did you obtain this property through the payment of money?'

From Marion's lips there was an immediate eruption of the most uproarious husky laughter that shook the entire room. 'No, you imbecile. I inherited all that you see!' With that Tom threw me a pompous smile that led me to believe that he could, in fact, see me, although Marion's eyes had so far remained closed throughout the entire conversation.

I continued to question Tom for a further 10 minutes and as far as I could ascertain by his rather cumbersome, mumbled responses, his full name was Thomas Sowerby, squire of the village. As far as he was concerned, the year was 1781 and the present occupiers of the building were trespassing on his property. Coincidently, research later confirmed not only the existence of the aforementioned Thomas Sowerby, but also that his father, Richard, was the proprietor of Dalston Hall in Cumbria, a location investigated by our team some 12 months earlier.

The gruff and rather arrogant persona of Tom gradually dissipated to be replaced by a much gentler, innocent presence. By observing Marion's body language, it became immediately apparent that we were now dealing with a very young child.

'Hello,' I offered warmly. Giggling, Marion tucked her legs up on the chair and began to fidget in a very convincing child-like manner. 'And what's your name?' I asked softly.

A shyly whispered reply tiptoed from Marion's lips. 'I told you, my name is Roseanne.'

A puzzled expression spread across her face as I explained to her that she couldn't have already told me her name as this was the first time we had ever met. Portraying signs of disappointment, she bowed her head and insistently repeated, 'I told you!'

'Okay,' I continued. 'Where was I when you told me your name? Was I in here?'

She shook her head. 'You were downstairs!'

A shiver ran down my spine. Had this child already made an attempt to talk to me earlier that evening and, if so, then why had Marion not picked up on her presence? She was, after all, supposed to be the medium.

'How old are you?' I asked.

Roseanne paused, gazing up at the ceiling. 'Five!' she exclaimed excitedly.

'Five? You're nearly all grown up!' I said playfully. 'Where's your mother?'

She looked towards the open attic door. 'She's downstairs.'

When I enquired about her father, Roseanne immediately lost her smile and hiding her face behind her knees, proceeded to curl up into a ball. It took a lot of persuasion to pull her out of her shell, but eventually she provided me with some relevant information that could be historically checked. An orchard was apparently her favourite place to play and according to her it lay, or used to lie, directly behind the pub by the lane where she used to live.

She could not give me any specific year, but our researchers did come across factual evidence of an apple orchard existing on the grounds up until the turn of the 19th century. Historical records also confirmed that the small road at the rear of the building was once called The Lane.

Our researchers worked for days sifting through every item of archive material relevant to each investigation, not an easy task even for the most enthusiastic historian. But in these early days of our working relationship I could not completely rule out the possibility that Marion may have researched all of these findings prior to the investigation. How on earth she could have achieved this without even knowing the location of a case beforehand, however, was a trifle baffling. This being the case, one had to ask the question: was she either an exceptionally knowledgeable historian or an exceptionally gifted medium?

As the séance continued, I was instructed by the team to press the girl for information regarding her father. This was a task that really did not appeal to me, but then again, the whole point of these investigations was to gather as much evidence and information as we possibly could and so reluctantly I agreed. Just as before, the moment her father was mentioned the child withdrew once again, only this time she began to sob. In short agitated breaths she blurted out, 'I don't like you any more,' sending a quiver of guilt through my conscience. My brother Graham indicated that she was portraying all the signs of an abused, frightened child and suggested terminating the link. So, calming her fears as best I could, I told her to go back downstairs to her mother.

My final question, 'Are we still friends?' went unanswered, as Marion's body language confirmed that Roseanne had left.

As if in a trance myself, I stared blankly at Marion, searching for some form of forgiveness, but to no avail. I muttered the words, 'Sorry, Roseanne,' under my breath in the vain hope that perhaps she could still hear me. Suddenly without warning, a blast of tingling cold air enveloped my entire body leaving me with an immense sensation of forgiveness, so strong it literally took my breath away.

Before I could report this cuddle, Graham whispered excitedly, 'Did you feel that?' I turned to him and nodded. Our researcher Suzie then announced that something relating to a cold blast had just passed by her, heading towards the stairs. Bar staff clearing up downstairs also felt an icy presence brush past them in the bar at precisely the same time, only on this occasion the incident produced feelings of amusement rather than fear.

During the remainder of the séance, several more visitors communicated with us through Marion, including a postman from the 1960s and a draper's wife hailing from 18th-century Hitchin who, accompanied by her husband, claimed to have only arrived at the inn the day before. Our final visitor that evening was a rather confused deaf and dumb servant girl who, despite making various attempts to communicate, left us on this occasion with more questions than answers.

Marion eventually awoke from her trance-like state, claiming to remember nothing of the events witnessed during the séance. Tired and drained, she took her leave of us and retired to the control room.

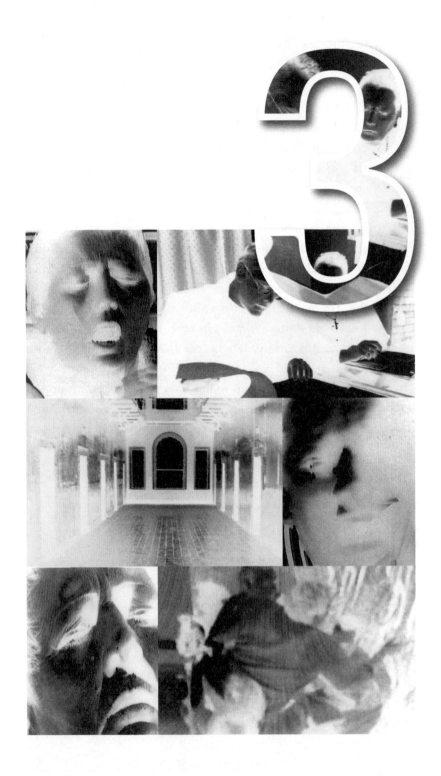

The Ghosts of Sowerby – Part 2

Despite all of the initial excitement, the following two nights at the Sowerby Arms revealed no further unexplained activity. Our infrared cameras and stills photographs produced images of nothing more than an empty pub, closed to the public and quietly left to indulge in dreams of future profit. By the fourth night, however, all of this was to change dramatically.

Night four

Before my departure from home, Sheila had telephoned me to say that she had witnessed something strange whilst housecleaning in the attic that afternoon and would brief me on my arrival. Marion had informed us that she would not be able to attend that evening and passed on her apologies and best wishes.

I entered the pub through the main entrance and from that moment on I began to sense something very familiar. My first port of call was the control room for a cup of tea and a team briefing where, shortly afterwards with all team members present, Sheila began to tell us her story.

That afternoon, she had been busy dusting prior to vacuuming the attic and in the process had accidentally knocked over a bowl of walnuts. Agitated, she bundled them all back into the bowl and was about return to her chores when from behind her, she distinctly heard a series of unusual clicking sounds. In the space of two seconds, a line of walnuts had been inexplicably placed across the entire length of the room in a line so perfect and evenly spaced that to offer any scientific explanation at the time would have proved fruitless. Alone and obviously afraid, she had backed away and locked the door behind her. The room had remained untouched since the landlady's encounter.

Stepping cautiously inside we found the aforementioned walnuts all residing in their proper place, in a bowl on the coffee table. Had Sheila made the whole thing up? If not, then perhaps a member of staff had dutifully cleared the floor, little knowing that in the process, he or she had unwittingly extinguished the only scrap of paranormal evidence that had so far come to light. On the face of it, this seemed impossible because Sheila owned the only set of keys for the locked door, and furthermore all members of staff claimed that they had not been anywhere near the attic all afternoon.

Unfortunately, as is generally the case in these situations, we only had the word of one individual witness who could provide no physical evidence to prove conclusively the validity of her claims. Nevertheless, the landlady remained extremely unnerved and as I watched her edging around the room she so obviously loved, I couldn't help but believe her. In an attempt to quash her fears, I explained that in most cases occurrences such as these were very rare indeed and that the likelihood of this happening again was extremely remote.

She asked me if I could sense a presence in the room, to which I replied no. Making my way back downstairs, I hoped she believed me, for under her present state of anxiety I thought it best not to mention that I could now sense not just one, but also a mass of concentrated static energy that seemed to bombard me persistently as I moved around the building.

Over the previous two nights, Marion had claimed to have felt a number of spirits shadowing her every move; now, with her absent, could they possibly be turning their attention towards me? The next few hours spawned a panic deep within me so unnerving that at one point I even contemplated leaving the investigation and returning home.

Marion and Andy in the Sowerby Arms attic

Mediums and clairvoyants claim that spiritual contact can only be achieved when an individual's psychic vibration level matches those given out by a spiritual entity. In other words, contact is a two-way process of telepathy between two consenting parties. Apparently, everybody's aura of energy vibrates at different levels depending upon the individual and, if true, this would explain why certain people claim to sense paranormal activity while others are left to reside in the background, watching with occasional envy and wonder.

It is said that lost or trapped souls are attracted to individuals who possess clairvoyant abilities in much the same way as a moth is attracted to light. For an experienced medium, this notion is routine.

Andy and Marion, the ghost detectives

For me, however, the very thought of ghosts hovering around my aura made me very uncomfortable. Recalling my crash course in psychic protection, I began to create this invisible barrier around me. I felt like an idiot, but within seconds the sensations of bombardment that I had endured since my arrival gradually began to subside. As I've already said, the theory of a psychic shield, a warm, brighter-than-light cocoon of pulsating, impregnable spiritual protection may be nothing more than the mind conquering one's own self-delusional imagination. But it worked.

Closing time

Around 9.30pm, the team congregated in the control room, little knowing that the Sowerby Arms was about to come to life. With Sheila's permission and much to the amusement of the staff, Graham began to hang Christmas decorations in the restaurant. Locals filtering through the restaurant heading for the toilets all made the comment that the ghosts wouldn't let them stay up there for long.

All infrared cameras were set and connections checked and rechecked before the remainder of our team headed back upstairs to the control room. Playing upon the theory that I had apparently established an empathy with the occupants, Graham suggested that I remain in the restaurant bar and report any unusual occurrences to the team via radio. Armed with a walkie-talkie, I made my way back down to the bar to join Sheila, who was hinting to her small band of regulars that their night in the pub was about to come to an end. At 11.45pm, the last remaining customer was finally persuaded to finish his drink and head for home. Once the pub was empty, I radioed the team informing them that we were ready to go and that the main door had been locked.

Sheila joined me behind the bar and began to gaze nervously through the serving hatch, surveying the restaurant that lay beyond. Telling her not to worry, I advised her to follow her normal routine and close down the pub as if I wasn't there. Nodding, she set about her duties. One by one the lights were switched off in both bars until finally the pub was drowned in semi-darkness. From my vantage point behind the bar, I surveyed the decorations that were hanging motionless in the restaurant.

It was an eerie setting, one that even Santa himself despite all of his 'ho, ho, ho's would have remained cautious of. The remainder of the room was barely visible through the shadowy gloom, but I logically reassured myself that if there was anything hiding out there in the dark then our infrared cameras would assuredly determine that it would not stay hidden for long.

Ten minutes passed by, until turning to Shelia to ask if there was any chance of a cup of tea, I suddenly realised that it was getting colder, a fact quickly confirmed as Sheila pulled her cardigan up around her shoulders.

'This is the way it always begins,' she muttered nervously.

'You don't have to stay down here, you know,' I offered.

'I'm all right,' she whispered. 'I've had to live with them for 28 years. Do you think they scare me now?'

Before I had a chance to reply the temperature suddenly plunged dramatically within a matter of seconds, leaving both Sheila and me to shiver, as an invisible, freezing cloud began to envelop the entire bar. Startled by my icy surroundings, my immediate reaction was to locate the gigantic fridge door that had opened itself up.

The landlady began to edge towards the stairway door, mumbling, 'They're here, they're here,' while I fumbled for my radio.

Wave upon wave of sheer static energy began to pass by and through my entire body, tingling every nerve ending in the process, until finally the realisation that we were no longer alone slowly began to dawn. Imagine for a moment that you can see yourself standing, eyes closed, in a busy underground station, with people endlessly brushing by you back and forth; and then throw in the illusion that you are standing in a freezer charged with static and you will be close to understanding the experience.

Sheila and I stood our ground as hordes of invisible entities moved through and around us as though they were strolling through the restaurant. The sensations indicated that they were heading in and out of the restaurant and my perception of this was confirmed when I noted that the decorations hanging in the dining area were no longer stationary. They were being tugged from below.

I literally could not believe my eyes. Excited and amazed, I radioed the team upstairs.

'Graham, it's all kicking off down here, can you please confirm that the decorations are moving, over?' There was a brief pause before my walkie-talkie crackled into life. 'My God,' Graham exclaimed, 'Yes, we can confirm. We have a perfect picture on monitor one and all video recorders are running. Are you two okay, over?' I reassured the team that Sheila and I were fine and that whatever was there appeared to have no interest in us at this stage.

From our hideaway behind the bar, we both watched fascinated as unseen hands appeared to be tugging the decorations, resulting in the sounds of twanging elastic as the streamers ricocheted off the ceiling in all manner of directions, refusing to succumb to any efforts of attack. The energy emanating from the restaurant was now so intense that I could feel the outer vibrations tingling my fingertips.

Once again I radioed Graham and advised him that if he intended to take any photographs then now would be a good time. Sheila meanwhile stood transfixed. Recovering her composure, she blurted out a question, not to me but to our guests:

'How many are there of you?' she asked firmly. I heard no answer, but the look on Sheila's face as she turned to me was sheer amazement. 'Eight,' she shouted, staring at me round eyed. 'Didn't you hear them? They said eight!'

Eager to discover more, I suggested that she ask them if they knew what century they were living in. This time the reply came to us both, not as a voice as one might expect, but through a thought, very similar to how an idea suddenly comes into your mind. In a stern, clear manner somebody replied, 'Madam, sir, do you know what century you are in?' Stunned as I was, I couldn't help but laugh because the whole notion was ridiculous, crazy and impossible!

The creaking of the stairs indicated that Graham was about to join us and sure enough, camera in hand, he appeared shivering in the doorway.

'Jesus,' he whispered. 'Just as you get halfway down the stairs, it's like walking into a bloody freezer!' The electrical sensations around us began to increase once again and Graham remarked that perhaps his arrival had provoked some kind of reaction.

'Look at that!' Sheila suddenly whispered, sharply. We all turned our attention to the restaurant. The decorations were now behaving in such an extraordinary fashion that the poor landlady decided that she had had enough and as she turned to leave she yelled back over her shoulder, 'Go ahead, pull them all down. See if I care!'

In a flurry of activity, the tinsel streamers began to twist themselves around and around, creating a kaleidoscope of light reflective colour that seemed to illuminate the splendour of the entire spectacle. We stared in silence, our own breath barely audible above the continual rustling of paper and tinsel as it continued its battle with the unseen assailant. Finally, amidst an array of flash photography and snapping sounds, the decorations fell one by one to the ground. In seconds, the modern-day majesty of Christmas had been transformed into a crumpled pile of tinsel and cotton.

In the blink of an eye the atmosphere returned to normal and all sensations abruptly ceased. Standing there in the gloom feeling somewhat overwhelmed, I managed a gentle nod of gratitude for having witnessed such a remarkable event. The restaurant still retained some of its former Christmas splendour, but only in the guise of natural trinkets such as holly and ivy, trinkets that in the 18th century would have been perfectly acceptable. The synthetic streamers, perhaps alien to that time, were strewn about the floor.

Nothing further happened that night. The next morning as dawn broke, the team gathered in the control room to review the video and photographic footage. The photographs taken prior to the collapse of the decorations revealed seven lights, positioned directly along one half of the felled streamer. Many alternative suggestions were put forward in order to explain why the synthetic decorations alone had been torn down. Maybe the weakening of sticky tape eventually brought them down or perhaps the vibrations from the floorboards as team members walked around in the rooms above were responsible. We had conclusively logged that no draughts or extraction fans were responsible, since all electrical appliances had been switched off (hence no tea). Additionally, there were no windows open in the vicinity prior to the vigil. The only remaining conclusion was difficult for the sceptics to accept. The case was closed and labelled 'Unexplained'.

Some days later, I returned to the pub and Sheila allowed me to inspect the three guest bedrooms. In every single room, I felt and located traces of energy exactly where guests had reported seeing some form of apparition. I discovered that the energy lines had an overlapping pattern. The fact that these lines were there obviously fuelled my fascination, but why they were arranged in such a graphic manner made absolutely no sense to me. It would, of course, be interesting to uncover the original blueprints of the building and even more delightful to discover that prior to some Victorian renovation, a large room had perhaps once stood in the space now occupied by three guest rooms. Maybe time will tell.

My belief in ghosts and the paranormal was divided back then and I made no great pursuit to possess any mediumistic abilities following this case. However, I soon found myself travelling down a new road of self-discovery that would ultimately leave me with considerably less scepticism than I had ever imagined possible.

Author's note: the location and names featured in this case have been changed.

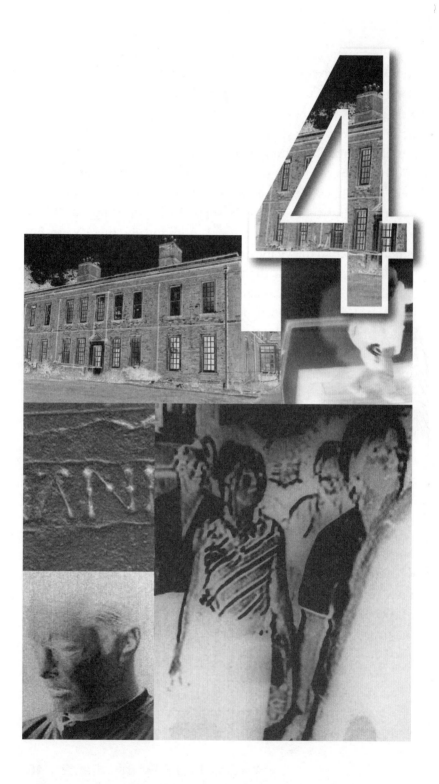

Alice and the Smoking Armour

The year 2001 had been an exciting one with the *Ghost Detectives* TV series, for it provided me with the opportunity to visit some splendid locations, soak up the history, get paid for the privilege and, if my luck prevailed, hopefully run into one or two extraordinary paranormal encounters.

Alice

The grounds around this stunning 17th-century manor house were vast, a seemingly impossible time capsule of beauty that greatly complemented the building situated at the centre of the landscape. It wasn't difficult to summon up images of the past, since many of the staff donned Victorian dress to add flavour to the ghost tours they conducted on a daily basis for members of the public. Bowden was a tourist attraction, and as such a doubt as to the validity of its alleged haunting was foremost on my mind. But as the sun set and darkness enveloped the scene, the serene atmosphere within the empty building began to subside.

It was 2am and as I walked the darkened corridors of the house that familiar sensation of being watched began to play with my subconscious. Despite the obvious expectations naturally associated with such an old building, the prim, clean interior of the house illuminated by the moonlit windows defied any subconscious thoughts I had of a ghostly presence. However, upon reaching the end of the landing corridor, the impression that I was being followed was now becoming more acute. Approaching the guest bedroom, which for the purposes of the investigation had become the base control room, the faint sound of a number of giggling children echoing back from down the hallway brought me to a dead stop.

I immediately radioed in to the two female members of the team who were stationed in another part of the house monitoring the CCTV cameras and enquired if anybody had giggled in the last few minutes. Their response was negative; all was quiet, nothing to report.

Looking back the way I had come, I forced myself to think logically. Here I was, alone in the dead of night in a supposedly haunted house with only my size eight shoes for company. Once I had ruled out the bizarre improbability that the giggling was the work of a trickster hiding somewhere in the house, I had to conclude that the real culprit had to be some kind of subconscious expectation. In layman's terms, my tired mind was playing tricks. Satisfied with this conclusion I turned to move away, but the moment my back was turned, a tingle began to roll up my spine as the sound of childish giggles returned, only this time much closer.

Turning around, I half expected to see a cheeky child standing before me, but this was 2am in a house where basic discipline would, I'm sure, be kept. In any case, the owners lived at Bowden with their elderly father and no children were in residence. I called out asking if there was anybody there. Apart from the wind whistling through the rafters in the attic above, there was silence. No movement. In fact, it was so quiet that I half-expected something to happen, such as a suit of armour to come to life or a picture to fly off the wall. But as the minutes ticked by, it became clear that nothing was lurking in the shadows except my imagination.

Now in the control room, I turned my attention to the task of replacing the batteries for the cameras and sat myself down on the edge of the bed, enjoying a swig of lukewarm tea from my flask. I closed my eyes as the sweet taste of Tetley warmed through me.

Bowden House

Leaning over to place the cup on the dressing room table I became aware in my peripheral vision of a movement to the left of me.

Turning my gaze, I became puzzled by a wobbling distortion, similar to the one that precedes a migraine headache, that appeared to float slowly across the bed. Then I was astonished to find myself face to face with a small girl, perhaps seven to eight years old, wearing Victorian dress.

This was the Holy Grail, a real apparition standing before me like something out of a dream. I never had time to pinch myself because she was only there for an instant, but in that time I registered the white ashen face, the blue frilly dress, jet-black hair and the piercing blue eyes that stared at me.

She stood motionless, gazing up at me displaying all the manner and authority of an adult, and for a moment I felt like a child about to be told off. Then in an instant I found myself staring at empty space that moments before had held her form. Shocked, excited and briefly panic stricken, my eyes began searching the area of the bed for any evidence of her visitation, but there was nothing. The figure had vanished into thin air.

Feeling an overwhelming sense of humbleness and gratitude, I gathered my thoughts and found myself thinking: did I really see that? Was that a ghost, or some kind of subconscious projection fuelled by simple wishful thinking? I felt none of the fear that one might expect. In fact, I had no time to digest what I had seen, for the apparition was there and gone in the blink of an eye, but the memory of that child's face is still clear. She had looked unwell, at death's door even, but strangely enough this was no misty ghost-like figure I had seen. She had appeared as solid and real as any living person would have looked standing before me that night.

The ghost of little Alice is a well-known story at Bowden House. The little girl died of tuberculosis in 1765 in what is now known as the Pink Room, and her ghost has appeared many times over the years to staff and visitors alike, mainly on the grand staircase. The question is: why does she still remain? Could it be that I had truly encountered the spirit of a girl trapped between worlds? Alternatively, perhaps the house simply contained a memory, a projection of residual energy held within the walls continually replaying a child's last days of life.

Later that week, a séance in the Great Hall attracted another of Bowden's lost souls. The full account can be read in Chapter 7, under the heading, 'Experiencing the séance'.

The case of the smoking suit of armour

It had been a long drive, over nine hours, and I remember the relief as at last we came to a stop in the grounds of Pengersick Castle situated not far from Land's End in Cornwall. The team consisted of six investigators, eager to explore the myths and legend of this 400-year-old structure.

Joining us on this case was renowned and respected ghost hunter Bob Snow, a man who had dedicated his life to the exploration of ghosts and hauntings. He was passionate about the castle, having visited the place before. On the journey down, he informed us that in his opinion, the chance of coming across such an active haunting as Pengersick was around a hundred to one. Great odds, great-looking place, but I remained passive and refused to allow any such stories to fuel my expectations of what might lay ahead.

Built around 1500, Pengersick, despite having legends of witchcraft and demonic practices attached to it, is probably one of the most charming places I have ever visited. It is believed that legends such as these were probably conjured up by smugglers to keep people away while they hid their ill-gotten gains on the site.

The castle itself has many ghost stories, the most poignant being the phantom image of a 14th-century monk seen walking the grounds along the exact route that historically matches the century he lived in; but by far the most haunted area in the whole place was reputed to be the master bedroom.

Over the years, investigators claim to have encountered strange orbs of light, electrical malfunctions and sudden temperature drops. Stories of demon dogs, a 13-year-old girl who danced to her death off the battlements, a young boy who tugs at ladies' dresses, a woman seen walking through walls, and a man strangled and stabbed to death in 1546 are just some of the spine-tingling tales that gave Pengersick the title of the most haunted castle in Britain.

With a castle so dominated by ghost stories, it isn't really the kind of place you would expect to find a sweet old lady living in. The owner, Angela Evans, who had more cats than Batman's female arch-enemy, was a no-nonsense, resourceful kind of a lady who had no real belief in ghosts or the haunting of her magnificent home.

The feeling that this would be a complete waste of time was evident all around, but we were here to make a television programme and for that reason alone, I put away my opinions and began to focus upon the job in hand. The small camera crew had arrived earlier that afternoon to film various exterior shots, together with our arrival scenes. Now, as night began to fall, work was focusing on the long, arduous task of rigging the castle's hotspots with sensory CCTV recording devices.

The team worked like a well-oiled machine and before long it was apparent that not even one of Pengersick's mice would successfully be able to sneak past in the dead of night without being captured on our ghost-cams – that is, assuming that Mrs Evans cats hadn't wiped out the whole population. By 10pm everything was in working order, all video units were on standby, trigger objects were set and, most importantly, the kettle was on. So off I went to take my first look at the alleged haunted bedchamber.

We are the knights who say, 'No smoking, please'

The room was certainly eerie and held an odour of old bedclothes long since laid out for display across the four-poster bed that dominated the ancient space before me. In the far corner stood an old wardrobe, strangely out of place despite its obvious use, and I half expected Dr Who to come bounding out of the doors at any moment in the guise of Tom Baker (who was narrating my series, *Ghost Detectives*).

Touring the room, I felt no sense of anything remotely unusual. It was just a quaint old Tudor-style bedchamber suspended in time for the wonderment of tourists. A ghost would have certainly felt at home there and furthermore I would place bets that certain people left alone by the bed in the dead of night would experience something untoward, as many witness reports over the years conclude.

However, whether ghosts abounded in Pengersick still remained to be seen. According to the castle legend, a man was murdered in this room by strangulation and stabbing — in which order is anybody's guess. Tales of witchcraft practices, such as the slaying of babies as they were born in the very bed that stood before me, didn't sway me at all from the belief that Pengersick, in my opinion, was about as haunted as my garden shed.

With the only manifestation present being my own disappointment, cries of astonishment resounding up from the room below snapped me out of my gloom and I headed for the door. The sound of surprise, fear and urgency were not something to be expected from a tired band of paranormal investigators on their first night unless, of course, one of the girls had perhaps encountered the last surviving mouse brave enough to step out into the open. On the other hand, the excited ruckus from below wasn't primarily female voices. Male ones were now joining in and as the *thump, thump* of panic in motion grew in intensity, I wondered if tiredness had given way to a full-scale punch-up.

Making my way down the stairway I had visions of many scenarios. Could it be that a real apparition had just walked through the wall for all to see or perhaps a poltergeist, driven half insane by our intrusion, was at this moment venting his wrath by hurling priceless artefacts and perhaps the odd cat at the team? As I reached the bottom of the spiral landing, our tall cameraman raced out in front of me like an Olympic athlete seeking a world record, heading in the direction of the car park.

The scene that awaited me in the castle room was similar to a chaotic scene from a Monty Python film. At first I couldn't understand what all the commotion was about, but as I spied the suit of armour standing by the far wall the whole situation became abundantly clear. Around the mighty knight's battle dress, a gentle mist was wafting up from the gauntlet, providing any onlooker with a suggestive view that they were witnessing the first stages of a ghostly manifestation.

The effect was certainly surreal and for a moment, as our cameraman barged by me with a new digital video tape already hastily ripped off its packaging and ready to load, I, too, stood transfixed, believing this to be authentic paranormal phenomena.

Bob, of course, was in his element, repeatedly stating to everyone present, 'I told you! Didn't I tell you that this castle is one of the most active hauntings in Britain?'

With his enthusiasm for the castle spilling over, I feared he may have a heart attack at any moment if he didn't calm down. Fortunately, he was pulled outside for an interview; but with only seconds to compose himself, the poor man only managed to deliver an unintelligible babble of stutters to camera before the director called for a second take.

I strolled back in to the centre of the mystery to discover the real truth behind the ghostly, smoking suit of armour. It was quite simple really. While setting up the base station, one of the team – realising to his horror that the castle was non-smoking – had hurriedly extinguished his cigarette in the only hiding place he could find nearby, namely the armour's glove. With the glove now off, two of the team were busy ensuring that the fire was indeed out and luckily, other than a few strands of scorched synthetic padding, no damage was evident.

The case had served as a prime example of how easy it is to get carried away in the midst of a haunted house. The culprit was on his first trip with us. He apologised and the matter was forgotten, although for health and safety reasons the person in question was never invited back. So ended the mystery of the haunted armour.

Conclusion

Haunted houses can conjure up many ghosts within the mind. Incidents mistaken for supernatural phenomena are commonplace and all paranormal investigators have at one time or another fallen prey to the obvious, having bypassed the facts. Later in this investigation, we were fooled again, this time by specks of dust illuminated by one of the film crew's lights that we all mistook for floating orbs. The only positive result that I recall from this case was an unusual temperature drop in the haunted bedroom that seemed to encircle an old-fashioned spinning wheel, together with a few more orbs located by local dowser Alan Neil that had to remain inadmissible as evidence, simply due to the amount of dust within the room.

At the conclusion of this case, I left Pengersick with the opinion that if there were indeed ghosts inhabiting the castle, they had all decided to take a week's holiday when we arrived.

The
Fly
Tower

Originally opened in 1787, the Theatre Royal in Margate is the second oldest theatre in Britain, boasting over 200 years of tradition and holding around 2,000 patrons. It has been the seat of repeated reports of various bangs, footsteps and ghostly screams that are told to echo across the stage before finally exiting through the stage door. Many believe the ghosts inhabiting the theatre to be poltergeists.

The ghosts were first reported by the local press in 1918, when the spectre of Sarah Thorne made her debut appearance. Reputed to be a martinet, Sarah Thorne managed the theatre until 1894 and on her death five years later the theatre soon went into decline, becoming a bingo hall and a cinema before reclaiming its original role as a working theatre in 1930.

Margate's Theatre Royal

Her spirit is rumoured to have come back to protest at the modern usage of the theatre and according to witness reports of the time, her anger was so extreme the local constabulary had to be called in on one occasion, but, of course, they found nothing. Many say that the theatre is teeming with restless spirits, including an actor who, having been sacked, apparently committed suicide by throwing himself from the box into the orchestra pit.

During the 1950s, assistant stage manager Howard Lee stated that the bolted main doors of the theatre would mysteriously unlock themselves sometimes twice in one hour and told how lights in the foyer refused to stay switched off. These incidents obviously created a lot of unease for the staff, but one brave witness by the name of Alfred Tanner refused to let any ghosts get the better of him.

The year was 1966 and Alfred had been employed to redecorate the theatre, agreeing to work through the night so as not to interfere with the shows played out during the day. It wasn't long before he began to hear whispering voices followed by footsteps that sounded as though somebody was walking towards him. Mr Tanner's bravery was exceptional because he stood his ground, continuing his work despite hearing heart-stopping noises in the dead of night, such as the box office door slamming by itself and a heavy thump by the front row seats. Even a bright orange ball of light that, according to his testimony, morphed into a human head as it strode across the stage did not deter him.

Over time, the number of ghosts stories associated with Margate's Theatre Royal has increased year by year, making it probably the most haunted building in Britain, for it seems that everybody who visits this fine old theatre leaves with a story to tell. One of the more modern spirits is by no means a vindictive poltergeist as long as she is acknowledged by the staff each morning. Auntie Pat, as she is affectionately known, used to be the theatre guide, and her love for the place was so strong that upon her death her ashes were placed in the wings of the theatre, marked by a plaque commemorating her work. Visitors have seen the ghost of this lovely, grey-haired lady on numerous occasions, and staff swear the theatre productions go more smoothly if you say good morning to Auntie Pat at the beginning of the day.

There is, however, one other more disturbing ghost to be found 15 metres/50 feet above the stage in what is known as the fly tower. Used by staff to rig lighting and curtain changes, the ascent to the fly tower is not for the fainthearted. Employees have felt not only the usual unease that at times is typical of the theatre, but also a strong presence of a man who can literally be nose to nose with you, causing many individuals to back away, run or on one occasion soil themselves on the spot. The identity of this frightening energy is unknown, although some say he was once a sailor whose ghost came with the timber salvaged from a ship to construct the upper levels more than 300 years ago. As we began our investigation in August 2001, little did we know that events were to take a terrifying turn for the worse once we crossed the threshold into the ancient mariner's domain.

As an actor myself, I had trod the boards in a variety of roles in the past and one never loses that adrenalin rush when walking out to an expectant audience for the first time. Feeling a nostalgic moment coming on, I stood alone on the Theatre Royal's stage gazing out at the vacant seats reliving my moments from *Oklahoma!*, *The Pirates of Penzance* and *No Sex Please, We're British*. The auditorium was like a palace, crimson red seats complemented by intricately patterned walls held in the Victorian atmosphere, preserving its past grandeur with all the dignity it so well deserved.

Closing my eyes centre of stage I could scarcely understand why anybody would be frightened by such a calm, golden place as this. Smiling to myself, I whispered the words, 'There is no way this theatre is haunted.'

The crashing sound that followed caused me to jump almost out of my skin. It had come from the wings, stage left directly underneath the fly tower (although since I had just arrived, the relevance of this didn't register because I had no idea where the tower was located). Half expecting to find a mountain of heavily stored scenery in a pile, I rushed over to the wings, a place where performers nervously await their curtain call, to find no trace or explanation for the booming noise just heard. The area was clear, the theatre empty and with the team due to arrive from the hotel any minute I began to wonder if my comments had enticed an early reaction from one of Margate Theatre Royal's many ghosts.

Auntie Pat's smiling face looked on from the confines of her portrait as the team set about the awesome task of rigging the theatre for the forthcoming investigation. Following the advice of the stage manager, we soon became accustomed to greeting Auntie Pat each morning, much to the amusement of my sceptical brother Graham who so far had been fairly unconvinced by any haunted house we had entered. Apart from a few dust particles illuminated by the stage lights, no evidence of paranormal phenomena came to light. The place was dead, although not in the way we had hoped.

On the fourth day, we all had time to relax, as the narrator of the series, Tom Baker, was called in to film his links on location. I remember that day passing well, with Tom on great form obviously enjoying himself between takes, cracking joke after joke with his own uniquely dramatic delivery. Asking him his thoughts on the paranormal over a cup of tea, he looked straight into my eyes and whispered, 'I don't believe in ghosts, but they do believe in me.'

By mid-afternoon, mediums Paul Hanrahan and Marion Goodfellow had agreed that our strongest chance of capturing any evidence was to run a séance in the fly tower. My feelings were divided between anticipation and caution, because by now we had all heard the stories from the staff and equally sensed a feeling of menacing unease (though no team member had as yet openly admitted it).

Tom Baker was wrapped and driven away by 9.30pm, leaving us a scant amount of time to arrange the filming of a séance so high above the stage. Producer/directors Mark and Paul from the Lion TV film crew took their leave, wishing us luck with whatever else we had planned and finally, with time to prepare, I scouted around for a nice quiet area within the theatre to compose myself. Something was going to happen, I could feel it biting into my intuitive thoughts, and as the clock ticked away the minutes to start time, our seemingly lacklustre approach to this case began to worry me more and more.

Summoning up my psychic barrier of protection usually took no more than seconds to achieve, but the situation here was different. I was scared and this time was taking no chances. Pushing away the illogical aspects of the protection procedure, I felt more relaxed having opted for a *you never know so beware* attitude, for if I were to face the anger that possessed the fly tower then I had to be ready to draw upon every scrap of my inner defences.

Terror in the fly tower

Four of the seven-strong team volunteered to take part, including medium Paul Hanrahan, myself and our researcher Suzie, whose role would be to take notes. Additionally, my brother Graham had agreed to be present to document the séance on video.

Marion's original plan of action was for us all to prepare ourselves in a mass prayer of protection, but time was against us and as we stood by the ladder leading up to the tower she turned to me, softly whispering a command for me to keep away.

Before I could respond, her hands grasped the rungs of the ladder and she launched herself skyward climbing with all the agility, speed and grace of a person half her age. Calling after her to stop, I clambered my way up behind her, shouting down to the others for assistance. Upon reaching the top I paused for a moment scanning the fly tower's dismal setting, before finally spying Marion through the railings. She was sitting on a chair by the far wall, eyes closed, rigid and alert. Carefully taking up a position opposite her, what immediately struck me as odd was her calm rate of breathing. Marion was not an agile person, she smoked too much, carried a fair amount of weight and was in her early fifties; so how on earth had she managed to ascend such a height so quickly and not be gasping for breath?

One look at her face told me she was in trance. But with no protection placed around her or the team, I feared that we were now facing a very dangerous situation and to make matters worse, that terrifying drop lay just a step away.

Taking up their positions either side of me, Paul, Suzie and Graham filled the air with concerned questions as to what had happened, which I acknowledged by a simple nod towards Marion.

'She's in trance,' muttered Paul. 'Join hands quickly, we need to protect her!' Before Paul had finished his sentence Marion's eyes snapped open staring straight through me, unblinking, unwavering

Marion lunges across the table (taken from the TV footage)

and whilst I searched the windows of her soul for some indication of recognition, the blank poker face stare confronting me confirmed to us all that the person behind the eyes was not Marion.

Concern turned to fear as the medium's body rose from the chair, hands reaching out threateningly towards me. Sensing an impending attack I sat back in my chair out of her range and, as suspected, her right arm lashed out, missing me by a whisker. As I stood fast, ready to dodge another attempted assault, she suddenly lunged forward across the table dividing us, reaching out to the hanging stage ropes located directly behind me.

With all four team members now trying to restrain her, it took all of my physical strength to prevent her toppling over the edge of the fly tower to face certain death on the stage below. Managing to wrestle Marion back down into the chair, her struggling suddenly ceased as her body went limp with submission. The mumblings

Marion reaches for the ropes (taken from the TV footage)

slipping from her lips were unintelligible, but her agitated mannerisms indicated that whoever had a hold of her was in desperate need of escape. For nearly a quarter of an hour, we had to block her way time and time again, as her panic-stricken eyes searched each and every corner of the confined space for a route to safety.

With patience and empathy we finally managed to calm down the spirit inhabiting her body, repeatedly promising that we meant it no harm. It was clearly a man, that much was obvious; but despite our questions, the only clue we had to his fate was his fear of ropes. Perhaps he had fallen to his death or been hanged for some crime committed in the distant past. Nobody really knew or cared under the present circumstances.

The team restraining Marion from falling on to the stage (taken from the TV footage)

One thing was certain: the man was excessively paranoid, which posed the problem of how we could persuade such an unstable character to leave Marion safely and head back to whatever reality he had descended from. Fed up with sweet talk, I tried a more authoritative approach, demanding he leave her immediately. The frightened figure shaking in the chair pointed upwards to the rafters mumbling in broken English something like, 'I didn't do it, not me, I didn't do it.'

Hanging above us from the ceiling, a rope noose, most probably a theatrical prop, seemed to be the cause of the problem, so balancing on a stool I ripped it down, leaving Paul to throw it on to the stage below. All at once Marion's body slumped forward, her head lolling gently on to the table. We carefully checked her for any injuries before taking Paul's advice and allowing her time to sleep it off. The séance was over, the spirit had left Marion; but as we were about to discover, whoever had possessed her was far from gone.

With the investigation now over, the process of derigging the theatre had commenced. Everybody was busy except Marion, who was resting in the control room with a large black coffee. She had no memory of the events in the fly tower, but was able to explain her lack of patience being the cause of all the drama. The spirit from the tower had connected with her by the base of the ladder and rather than waiting as she should have done, curiosity took over, resulting in the energy catching her completely off guard. The entity, rather than lingering around her aura as invited, passed directly into the body, instigating a state of immediate trance, allowing the ghost free movement once again in a physical form. Some call this state a possession, where a spirit takes control of a human body by force, but in Marion's case there was an invitation, not an intrusion. However, the result had been a sinister experience for all involved.

Catch me if you can

Complaining that he felt a little strange, nobody noticed Graham's once confident persona begin to change because we were all tired and looking forward to making last orders in the pub next door. It had been a long week and the dramatic events in the tower had drained us all, so the last thing we needed was the unexpected to jump out at us once again. However, without warning all hell broke loose.

'Graham! Graham, wake up!' The sound of my brother's name being shouted in such an alarming manner brought me to his side in seconds. He stood motionless, frozen, eyes wide open, his camera tripods clattering to the stage as his grip and consciousness slipped away. Again as before with Marion, one look into his eyes was enough to know that the entity had entered him. Just how long it had been buzzing around his aura waiting to slip inside was unknown, but recalling how difficult the situation had been with Marion, I began to yell, threatening the ghost with demands that he should leave – in no uncertain terms!

Helpless, I could only watch as Marion and Paul, assisted by Joy Henson (who had remained in the control room with the rest of the team) encircled him and slowly drew the invading energy out. In seconds it was over, Graham blinked once then twice, before leaning on Paul's shoulder in a state of utter confusion. Marion immediately ordered Graham out of the building, warning us all that the entity was once again free to roam and could at any point attempt to enter any one of us.

Still reeling with the shock of seeing my brother in such a state of helplessness, I followed everyone else's example, nervously searching the wide, open theatre for any sign of the evasive ghost without taking the time to realise after all these years that they are invisible.

'Everyone on their guard,' whispered Marion. 'He's still around us, I can feel him.' A sudden blast of freezing cold air enveloped me and for a moment I visualised the spirit trying in vain to break through my defences. He was a wiry young man with a terrible complexion, his face pitted with acne, most likely from scurvy if he had indeed once been an ancient mariner. Realising he couldn't get to me, I smiled, promising never to doubt my training for psychic protection again. He was gone as quickly as he had arrived, breaking away from my vicinity and heading off in the direction of the control room.

'It's gone this way!' I yelled, running into the control room area to find Pauline, another of our team, staring blankly ahead in exactly the same state that Graham had been in moments earlier.

'Right,' said Marion, 'let's end this now.' Poor Pauline sat perched on the edge of her chair, face blank, nobody home except what lay hiding within her. 'One, two, three, out!' called Marion, snapping her fingers. Pauline came back to her senses, wondering what all the fuss was about, as the entity, now evicted for a third time, began to tire.

The silence of the theatre added to the anxiety of the team, as each member looked to another in turn, checking for any signs of change. Everybody appeared to be okay – a little shaken up but otherwise fine.

Graham never returned that night, opting instead for an early night at the hotel, but how he could sleep after that was beyond me. He told me he could still feel the entity around him for hours afterwards. But Marion pointed out there was no need for concern, because this feeling was only a form of residual energy, comparable to the scent left by a woman wearing strong-smelling perfume after a date.

That night, a lot of people's opinions changed within the team, none more so than my brother whose scepticism had taken a beating from his first real paranormal experience. In the space of just four hours, we had lost a large percentage of doubt and for those team members who continued their path investigating the paranormal,

Margate Theatre Royal would remain the pinnacle of their time exploring the unknown.

I didn't sleep that night. Even three large brandies had no effect, so I decided to rise early to welcome in the new day. My brain was alight with unanswered questions, for I had been witness to something so absurdly frightening that the decision to leave the paranormal field was once again foremost on my mind. However, with that fear came strength, an understanding of just how scary the unknown can be to the inexperienced mind. The mind: could it all really be happening in there? Were we all witness to nothing but expectation, a case of group hysteria? The cobwebs in my head needed sweeping away and with a light wind heading in from the south, I made my way down to Margate's solitary beach.

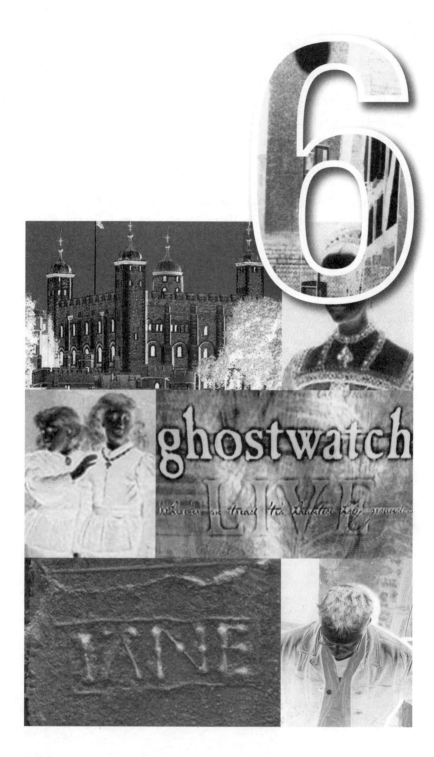

The Tower of London

John Stow once wrote during the reign of Elizabeth I: 'The Tower of London was a citadel to defend or command the city, a royal palace for assemblies or treaties, a prison of state for the most dangerous offenders; the only place of coinage for all England ... the armoury for war-like provision; the treasury of the ornaments and jewels of the crown; and general conserver of the most records of the queen's courts of justice.'

Begun by William the Conqueror in 1078 and completed in 1097, the Tower of London was constructed to protect and control the city of London and is today probably the most recognised, allegedly haunted building in the world. Over the centuries, the Tower has been witness to many a harsh judgement, encompassing imprisonment, torture, murder and executions, including the beheading of two of Henry VIII's wives, namely Anne Boleyn on 19th May 1536 and Katherine Howard on 13th February 1542.

Tower of London

Lady Jane Grey, the nine-day queen

Lady Jane Grey, great-granddaughter of Henry VIII, was born in the autumn of 1537, the daughter of Henry Grey and Lady Frances Brandon, the Marquees of Dorset. At just 18 years of age, in 1553 she was crowned nominal queen of England for a total of nine days in an unsuccessful bid to prevent the accession of the Catholic Mary Tudor.

Lady Jane Grey

However, Mary Tudor had widespread popular support and by mid-July even her own father had abandoned Jane and was attempting to save himself by proclaiming Mary queen. When Mary came to power she imprisoned Jane, her husband and her father in the Tower of London. While her father was pardoned, Jane and her husband Guildford were tried for high treason and sentenced to death. After her death, Jane's body was laid to rest in the Tower's Chapel and it is said that she still walks the grounds to this day.

The Princes in the Tower

The Princes in the Tower were Edward (1470–83) and Richard (1473–83), the sons of Edward IV and Elizabeth Woodville.

The Princes in the Tower

Edward had come to the throne as a result of the War of the Roses, but died suddenly in 1483 and the boys were passed over into the care of their uncle Richard. With the young Edward next in line for the throne, they were moved to the Tower of London where they took up residence. However, their jealous Uncle Richard declared the brothers illegitimate, because it was alleged that their father was contracted to marry someone else before his marriage to Elizabeth Woodville. In July 1483, Richard Duke of Gloucester got his way and was crowned Richard III.

The two boys were never seen again. The common theory is that their uncle had ordered them to be smothered in their sleep and buried within the very walls of the Bloody Tower. Whatever the truth may be, ghostly sightings of the two princes have been reported by more than one Tower guard throughout the centuries.

'Ghost Watch LIVE'

Home to the crown jewels, the Tower is guarded day and night by elite special forces, ever ready to repel and if necessary shoot on sight anybody who dares to trespass on to the queen's property. Never before had the crown granted permission for any paranormal investigation of any kind to be allowed within the fortress and as such the Tower's ghosts had remained a mystery, evolving into a concoction of bedtime stories and hushed up witness accounts that seemed likely to remain locked away behind the great doors of the Tower of London for ever. Until one day in 2001.

Having just completed filming *Ghost Detectives*, news came that the BBC had invited the team to take part in a TV programme entitled *Ghost Watch LIVE*. The job, which came as a big surprise, was to investigate the Tower of London's ghosts and, if possible, try and capture some kind of scientific evidence to prove their existence. Of course, everybody was excited as this was the first time such an investigation had been allowed to take place within the fortress. I had my reservations though, for the Tower is known worldwide as a tourist attraction and its ghostly tales of Lady Jane Grey and the two princes wandering around scaring the pants off anyone who dares to venture alone there at night were, to me, a little sensational. I really expected to find nothing at all.

The strength of a good paranormal investigator is to always cross-question yourself, because if you dig deep enough you will generally find yourself scrutinising your evidence. There's always a little flicker in the back of the mind that says, 'Go on, admit it: there is another explanation.' Whether or not you follow your instincts and look for that alternative answer is up to you. You cannot accept a ghost story as fact simply because somebody tells you it is true; first you have to experience or witness it. My philosophy has always been this: so okay, this building has a ghost, but until it makes itself known to me personally it doesn't exist.

However, as I soon discovered, the Tower of London's reputation for being haunted was, to say the least, a little understated. Many strange occurrences had been reported by the BBC team prior to the actual event. During pre-production, equipment would inexplicably break down and on repeated occasions whenever the researchers were examining historical facts on Lady Jane Grey, the computers would go haywire, although when checked by the IT technicians they were found to be in perfect working order. The

The BBC *Ghostwatch* logo

Tower's reputation was intimidating for many. In fact, a number of the BBC crew who were sceptical about ghosts admitted to feeling a little unnerved about entering the Tower, although few could openly explain why.

The sheer size of the place was daunting, yet despite a gruelling chain of TV and radio interviews leading up to the investigation, tiredness soon gave way to wonder, as with each step I found myself entranced by the majesty and timeless beauty of this historic structure. Accompanied by my fellow ghost detectives and a team of highly qualified BBC personnel, I had just two days and nights to explore the murky legends that lay hidden within the age-old walls. As darkness fell on night one, the team and I found ourselves standing on Tower Green with the knowledge that for security reasons alone, we would be locked inside the Tower with no chance of leaving until 6am the next morning. With all the rigging of CCTV night vision cameras and recording equipment set up, it was soon time to begin.

The Bloody Tower

The first impression I had was that someone or something wanted me to go to the Bloody Tower. The urge was a kind of calling that at the time was something I had never experienced, let alone understood; but my instinctive desire to explore and follow my heart led me across the green to face the awe-inspiring sight of London's most infamous place of torture. I had limited knowledge of what had gone on in this place and found myself relying on the history lessons I had paid little attention to at school, which wasn't much help.

Entering the ground floor of the Bloody Tower where Sir Walter Raleigh was interned by James VI of Scotland for 12 years, I stopped, somewhat amused by somebody's lack of respect, because following a heavy lecture from the Tower guards earlier that day, no smoking was top of the list when the rules were read out. Turning around to find the culprit, I was met only by the puzzled expression of my cameraman, shrugging his shoulders in bemusement.

The story goes that once you enter the Tower, the smell of pipe tobacco will eventually waft around the nostrils, and over the years many tourists had claimed to have witnessed the alleged aroma of Sir Walter Raleigh's bad habit. But this wasn't the past we were standing in, this was the here and now and no one was present in this part of the building except myself and one other. Yet there it was: a crusty old potent smell of a pipe burning.

Despite Raleigh's conviction for plotting against James VI in 1603, his internment quarters that lay displayed before me indicated that his standing in Elizabethan society had apparently rewarded him with moderate comfort, as opposed to the likes of Guy Fawkes and other such criminals who had endured barbaric agonies in the torture cells for their heinous crimes. With Raleigh's first death sentence reduced to imprisonment, he once again defied James VI in 1618 and was consequently executed on 29th October 1618, leaving behind him a legacy of tobacco and potatoes.

By the time I turned towards the Tower stairway, the tobacco odour had mysteriously vanished, leaving no remnant hanging in the air as one might expect. Motioning the cameraman to follow, I slowly began my way up the ancient, dimly lit spiral stairway, occasionally allowing my hand to brush against the brickwork laid by hard-working Elizabethan craftsmen who had long since died, totally ignorant of the eternal contribution they had made to British heritage. The air was still as we both shuffled our way around the cone-shaped structure, our footsteps echoing in the dark with each step ascended. As we neared the top, I began to sense something ahead.

I was staring straight at it but could see nothing. However, the static electricity I could feel buzzing through my being, together with that soft velvet of cool, dense air, was unmistakable and instantly recognisable. Standing before me hidden from my psychical realm was a ghost, the stranded energy of a life long ago and from what I could ascertain, the phantom seemed more afraid of me than I was of it. Carefully, I slipped my hand into my jacket pocket to collect my digital camera, but whoever this was saw through my stealth because all sensations suddenly ceased. The energy had moved and since I hadn't felt it pass me then I concluded that it had retreated back the way it had come. I moved forward two, three, four steps, and then began to quicken my pace as I realised that this spirit was on the run.

To my cameraman's surprise I gave chase, hurling myself up the last remaining stairs in pursuit, not caring for the heavily laden VT operator trying to keep up behind me. I quickly found myself out in the open, pausing as I came to a stop on the Raleigh walkway and as I tasted the fresh night air once again, the energy I had been chasing turned to face me. It was a girl, perhaps 14 years old and she was screaming at me to keep away.

I couldn't see her in a three-dimensional form the way we see ourselves. She was like a thought, a dream image intermixed within a wakeful state. I called for her to relax, convincing her that I meant her no harm, which appeared to do the trick until I took a step forward. In an instant she was gone, vanished together with the sensations that had accompanied her presence.

I had managed to take one photograph that revealed an orb of light floating on the walkway, which at the time was a big thumbs-up success, but since orbs are now known to be a result of dust and light reflection or regarded as simple common faults, especially with early digital cameras, I now look upon that photo with less conviction. However, my compassion was to lead me back there the next night, because I could not bring myself to leave without trying to find out who she was and, more importantly, help her if she would allow me to.

The Beauchamp Tower

The live show broadcast on UKTV involved an hour of running back and forth for interviews and listening to the same old rehashed ghost stories told in a somewhat eerie manner by actor Paul Darrow. As expected, no paranormal activity was captured during the show, but with the camera crew now on stand down, I decided to take a look at the Beauchamp Tower and enlisted fellow investigator Pauline Wall and presenter Danny Wallace to accompany me. Yet another stone spiral staircase awaited us behind the main entrance door and we began our ascent chatting about the view from our hotel rooms at the Tower Hotel and meeting Sir Cliff Richard

The ball of light photographed on the Raleigh walkway

earlier that night while he was enjoying a private tour of the chapel. We were about a third of the way up when I unexpectedly encountered what I can only describe as a force field.

We have all felt the power of a force field generated by two magnets opposing one another. Well, imagine that power in front of you barring your way and you will understand the surprise I felt. We could walk forward, but it made us dizzy and a little disorientated. Pauline commented that she felt she was being pushed back and Danny stated that he felt dizzy and off balance.

In this kind of situation, your logic has to be put to one side. I had opted to go back for some sensory electronic equipment, but instead opted to press on. If there was something there, we had to ensure that whatever it was understood that we meant no harm or malice. Advising everybody to switch off all cameras, we made our way to the top of the tower with virtual ease, where we found absolutely nothing, no sensations, no temperature drops. All we got was an orb or two on Danny's right arm before the batteries in the camera drained after taking just two photographs.

Feeling a little disheartened and with time on my hands, I paid a visit to the cell of the infamous nine-day queen, Lady Jane Grey. It was disconcerting to stand in the same surroundings once occupied by a former queen, untouched for over 400 years and, despite the knowledge that these walls had seen many a poor soul praying in their last hours before execution, the silence and calmness was surprisingly comforting. I began to wonder whether it was Jane I had encountered on the Raleigh walkway earlier that night, lost and afraid, perhaps cursed to relive her final moments in fear of death.

Standing alone in her last abode, I could only imagine what terror and betrayal this young girl must have felt, knowing that her brief life was to be cut short before she had even had the chance to live it. The cell was dark and foreboding, and would easily destroy a person's soul after time, trapping their senses behind the stone wall of this royal façade. Although I knew I could leave whenever I wished, the name 'Jane' etched into the cell wall by either the lady herself or her distraught husband Guildford Dudley as they awaited death still haunts me to this day.

The girl on the walkway

The following night, I teamed up with my brother Graham and since all was quiet we took our leave of the cameras and headed back up to the Raleigh walkway. Retracing my steps from the night before, I began telling him the story of my encounter with the mysterious girl, when unexpectedly within a matter of seconds a massive electrical charge surged through both our bodies simultaneously. Instinctively, we took two steps back, putting some distance between us and whatever had hit us.

Reaching out slowly with my hand, the rush of energy connected with me once again, only this time I recognised it as surely as I would have acknowledged an acquaintance's face. It was the girl: she was back. Sensing her between us, I asked Graham quickly to take a photograph and a small bright orb, roughly the size of a golf ball was captured directly in front of my chest. This particular anomaly was a little bizarre because this time I had

Lady Jane Grey's name engraved into the cell wall

directed the photographer to the exact place where energy had been sensed rather than taking a chance shot in the dark.

The notion that orbs are spirit disincarnate has always been for me a little farfetched. However, on this occasion something was felt by two independent witnesses at the same time, resulting in a picture that I still ponder about to this day.

I make no claims to be a medium, but with Marion's absence from this investigation I decided to use the limited knowledge I had available to attempt further contact with the girl in the hope of possibly finding out who she was and why she was there.

I opted for no cameras to film this, simply due to my lack of confidence as a medium. I had been under tuition from Marion for

The orb photographed on Andy's chest

over a year at this stage, but had never felt quite at ease with the work. The process of opening up your psyche is one thing and it is amazing what you see, feel and sense; but the problem I had was that I had not yet mastered the process of how to close down and switch it off.

Andy facing the Raleigh walkway

As I settled myself down on the walkway, I wished that Marion was here to help and guide me through this, but the BBC had been quite adamant that we use their own medium, Judy Farncombe. (She told me later that she too had picked up similar feelings of an angry young girl whom she perceived to possess a tremendous dislike of women.)

I sat cross-legged on the cold floor closely watched by my brother and one of the girls from the Tower's tourist information department. Closing my eyes, I began the process of opening up, clearing my mind, and then inviting whoever was there to come forward and communicate. Tentatively, I enquired if she knew what the year was and as the seconds passed with no response I began to feel a little out of place. I asked again only this time assuring her that I meant her no harm. Eyes still closed, I could now sense the atmosphere around me change as her emotional state began to calm itself and in my mind's eye I could see her shape nervously emerging from the safety of the shadows. It was then that I got my answer.

Oddly enough, considering the age and history of the place, the year that came to me was not what I would have expected. If it was imagination or wishful thinking I would assume that my subconscious would have picked a year such as 1579 or something similar, but what I actually got was 1974! Not really a year that stands out significantly in the Tower's long and bloody history, or so I thought.

She told me her father was an employee of the Tower and that they lived on the grounds. Apparently she had died in an accident on the stairway, although she could not remember quite what happened. This all came to me in a second, a flash of inspiration. The minutes passed. I had interaction, but was so dumbstruck I couldn't think of any more to ask. Blindly, I asked her name and her age, which emerged to be 14, but frustratingly no clue to her identity was forthcoming.

Throughout this subconscious interaction, I questioned not only my abilities but also the true nature of where these thoughts were coming from. Could it be possible that I was doing it, really talking to the dead or was this all just an imaginative fantasy? Following the procedures given by my teacher, I closed down as best I could before relaying the information to the tour guide standing shivering in the moonlight, her face a clear expression of nervous unease.

The guide informed me that the row of houses adjacent to the Tower were, in fact, used as resident homes for employees and their families and requested that we not report on TV any of our experiences regarding this young girl. I had no idea why she should request this, but she admitted to me that the year 1974 and the information I had picked up was very relevant. Disappointingly, she offered no further information, implying that I had uncovered something here that was confidential. I could do nothing but respect her wishes, and when interviewed later by Danny Wallace, I reported no unusual occurrences.

This was back in 2001 and as I look back I still wonder what the big secret was and if there was indeed a young girl's death, why was it covered up? As I later discovered, the year 1974 *was* significant in the Tower's history, a fact at the time I had no knowledge of. Below is the BBC's press announcement from that year:

1974: Bomb blast at the Tower of London

An explosion in the Tower of London has left one person dead and 41 injured. A bomb ripped through the Mortar Room in the White Tower at 1430 BST. The small basement exhibition room was packed with tourists from the UK and abroad who took the force of the blast. Many people suffered badly damaged and lost limbs and severe facial injuries. At least two of the victims were children and are being treated in St Bartholomew's Hospital.

Conclusion

Despite over 20 BBC crew assisting us in monitoring the Tower of London for two days and nights, no paranormal evidence was captured on film, apart from one or two light anomalies, one of which turned out to be a piece of dust caught in a draught by an infrared CCTV camera.

The unexplained force field in the Beauchamp Tower remains a mystery, as does the identity of the young girl on the Raleigh walkway. Whoever she may have been, we felt it best to help her and in the end, assisted by Judy Farncombe, her spirit was released, leaving me with a feeling of conclusion to the experience.

Many people present on this investigation had their own tales to tell. Some claimed they had feelings of being watched, others that they had heard screams, moans and whispers when alone in certain parts of the complex but with no evidence to back any of this up, all of these accounts, including my own, have to fall into the category of inconclusive witness evidence. I would love to return to the Tower someday with a smaller team to investigate the place properly without the restrictions of live TV because I feel there is evidence locked within the structure just waiting to be discovered.

Some may call them ghosts, others name them as ghouls. Whatever your preference, there are certainly echoes of the past still locked within those walls, perhaps eager to tell us their stories of the Tower of London.

Living
with
Ghosts

Gently tucking the bedclothes around her sleeping child, the woman paused for a moment, taking the time to check the rise and fall of her son's small chest ensuring that all was well before switching off the bedside lamp. The room had only recently been decorated and all traces of its former use as a storeroom were now gone, replaced by cartoon boats and rockets that travelled their way around the four walls in a spiral of animated fun.

Checking her watch, the mother moved to the window, gazing out at the fields beyond in relaxed satisfaction that for once, time was on her hands. The stars shone brightly, the summer air was warm and it seemed nothing could ruin the perfection of this night.

'I thought you were dead.' The soft gentle words of a very young girl sliced through her like an icy knife bringing forth goose bumps, the like of which she had never seen. For a moment the woman stood transfixed, shocked into disbelief at what she had just heard. Alone and confused, it took only seconds for her to conclude that the voice had materialised out of thin air.

Her mind racing, she recalled the unexplained events from the past two weeks as they flashed back into her memory, the footsteps, the bathroom taps turning themselves on and the ever-present sensation of being watched all began to assemble into a chilling realisation: the house she loved so much was haunted.

On the face of it, this case appears to sound like a routine witness report and indeed I would have treated it as such if it had not been for the fact that the woman in question was my wife and the aforementioned house my home. We were a young couple expecting our second child and had lived happily in our new home for over two years without any indications of unusual phenomena. So why a ghost should suddenly start to haunt us was beyond my level of understanding at the time. At this stage in my life, my interest in the paranormal was minimal, with any future ambitions as a ghost hunter lying unearthed in the depths of my mind. My son's bedroom felt quite normal, so we put the whole experience down to imagination and decided not to mention it again – until the day my gold watch went missing.

My work as a council housing officer had its pressures and following Christmas week the office was knee deep in unfinished work, so to wind down on a Friday night, I treated myself to a late film. My wife had gone to bed and it wasn't long before I, too, began to nod off. Determined to remain awake to see the end, it is possible that the following event was no more than a lucid dream.

There was no shimmering apparition or orb-like lights, just a young child who appeared, standing in the middle of my front room, barring my view of the television. She had her back to me, but the image was clear enough to note that she was in school uniform, grey jumper, skirt, white socks and black shoes.

Rubbing my eyes suspecting some lethargic hallucination, to my surprise, the apparition remained constant for at least five seconds before vanishing, together with my watch. Passing spirits can account for many reported hauntings that start for no apparent reason then suddenly cease just as abruptly. These cases are thought to be the result of roamers, ghosts who drop by for a nosey look around before travelling on elsewhere. Roamers enjoy the free movement and will to go where they please when they please. These entities don't belong anywhere and feel no attraction to any one particular place, as opposed to a haunting, where the spirit is attached to a building or place.

In the case of my wife hearing a little girl's voice saying, 'I thought you were dead', I believe that once the child had realised that my wife was very much alive and could not parent her in any way, she moved on. I just hope that one day she returns my watch.

Soon after, I began to work alongside a paranormal investigation team where I met up with my good friend Marion Goodfellow and a year or so later we became TV's *Ghost Detectives*. Midway through filming the series, we took advantage of a sunny weekend off and my wife invited us all round for a Chinese meal in the sun.

We had all enjoyed an afternoon of sunshine and as the day came to a close Marion motioned me to her side for a private word. According to her, a man was in the garden. Stupidly thinking we had an intruder, I began to look around for any sign of an uninvited guest. Rephrasing her statement, she told me there was a ghost, a large, gentle, friendly man who had been with us all afternoon, adding that he was more connected to the garden than the house.

The next day, I tentatively approached my neighbour who had been a resident in the village for over 30 years and enquired about the previous tenant. He described a huge man, gentle in nature, who adored children, despised nonsense and loved his garden. Back in the good old days, all the neighbours in the village knew and respected one another, and old Bill was liked by all. The gardens had been his pride and joy, and following his mother's death he spent his remaining years alone. Why this lovely old man who had risked life and limb dodging bullets in the Second World War finally ended his own life by hanging himself in what is now my garden shed remains a mystery.

Although we understood that a suicide is not suitable news for a housewarming party, we were nevertheless shocked and a little dismayed why nobody had told us this before now. However, rather than causing us any distress the possibility that we were sharing our home with a ghost never fazed us and why should it? He had been here long before us and I wasn't about to attempt his removal, for what right could I possibly have to demand he leave? Respectfully, I explained that this was now my house, a place for my wife and children. Nothing more needed to be said. Marion had been right about the ghost in the garden and the description she gave that afternoon perfectly matched the stature and personality of this man provided by my neighbour.

Experiencing the séance

For many years I had watched mediums conduct séances in haunted houses and always wondered what the experience entailed, so when the opportunity arose in August 2001 I grabbed it with both hands.

For the first time ever I was to take actual part in a séance to be held in Bowden's reputedly haunted great hall. There were no nerves, because the excitement far exceeded any feelings of fear and besides I would be alongside Marion Goodfellow, whom I trusted. She was like a mother to me. Fellow medium Paul Hanrahan would also be present.

Stretching across the oak floors encompassing the ground floor, the great hall was aptly named, incorporating delightful artefacts from bygone years that decorated the renovated structure of the wood-panelled walls. Taking pride of place at the centre of the hall stood a vast dining table that even Henry VIII would have felt at home with. In Tudor times, the house owned by the landed gentry was immense boasting three times its actual size today and housing a multitude of servants, lords and ladies. Following the Second World War, Bowden had operated as a children's home, before finally being saved from demolition in the early 1960s.

The house had seen more than enough living history to warrant a possible haunting, and as the time came for the séance to commence, I wondered if the night would encourage some of Bowden's oldest residents to return.

Following a short prayer, the three of us were seated in a circle by the grand fireplace and I listened with anticipation as Marion instructed me that if any energy came close to me during the séance, I was not to hold on to it but push it away so that it could connect with an experienced medium, namely either herself or Paul. My job was clear: I was there to observe, not practise mediumship. To build up enough energy for the ghosts to take part, first we all held hands as Marion began to channel our own natural energy around the circle, creating a kind of psychic electrical circuit. The theory is that the stronger the energy, the stronger the connection.

Subtly at first, a sensation of static electricity began tickling my fingers, increasing in intensity with every passing second as the flow of energy passed from Marion, up my right hand, down my left before exiting via my left hand to flow into Paul. Not really expecting to feel anything beforehand, I was pleasantly surprised to discover the whirlpool of power racing through my body, spinning the circle ever faster like some crazy top-speed rollercoaster ride. At its zenith, the acute sense of my surroundings became abundantly irrelevant, a blur of reality overshadowed by the spotlight of a completely new experience.

Suddenly the journey stopped. The feeling that I had perhaps fallen into a kind of self-hypnotic trance or maybe slipped into a dreamy sleep during the séance was the only explanation my senses had to offer. Searching for some rational explanation in the midst of the scene confronting me was impossible to contemplate, for the great hall no longer held any psychical characteristics of the 21st century. It was still a Tudor room, but in Tudor times. Even more bizarre, although we had started the séance not 10 minutes ago, it had been night, yet now the sun was shining through the windows.

The Bowden House séance

Time-slip phenomenon was something I had heard of but scarcely ever believed in. Witnesses who claim to have been transported forwards or backwards in time, if only for an instant, before returning to the present with vivid descriptions of past or future events were, in my opinion, far more engrossed in science fiction than reality. The theory sounded so ridiculous that I never thought for a moment that it could happen to me, but here we were, seated in a room in the 17th century.

Our circle remained unchanged. Paul and Marion were there, as was the candle that strangely enough still illuminated the room despite the daylight outside. My fascination was cut short as suddenly my attention focused upon the main door. Beyond it, the sound of footsteps could be heard approaching and with my eyes firmly centred on the Tudor door handle, I watched as it began to squeak and slowly turn.

A middle-aged lady dressed in a magnificent, ornately designed dress strode into the hall. Regal in pose, she came to a halt by the window pausing a moment before seating herself to its left. Silently, she gazed out across the courtyard outside as if waiting in anticipation. Her sadness was obvious, like an ever-expanding cloud filling the room and reaching out to me. My mind raced as her emotions slowly merged with mine, aware of the lump in my throat indicating an imminent flow of tears. Was this the way a ghost communicates, by giving themselves identity through some emotional psychic connection with the living? Was she trying to tell me her troubles or was I unknowingly reading her thoughts? All of these questions bombarded my brain simultaneously. Noticing my predicament, Marion squeezed my hand, assuring me that the emotions were not mine to keep, and with that I closed my eyes, allowing Marion to take over.

The ghost was crying, her sobs choking forward in breathless rasps from the very pit of her tortured soul. With Marion now deep in trance, I wondered if this could be the infamous grey lady often reported to be seen staring out of the window awaiting news of her missing son, Neville, lost at sea over 400 years ago. The sobbing figure certainly matched the story, but the dress was far from grey, displaying colours of white, mauve and blue. The light within the hall soon began to dim and with its decrease the figure of the lady began to blur. My eyes snapped suddenly open as if waking from a dream. Day had become night in an instant and all trace of the lady and the pleasant sunny Tudor morning had now vanished, replaced by the more recognisable décor of modern day. We had returned from over the rainbow and although I felt a twinge of disappointment, I was more than happy to snap back to my own reality.

During the great hall séance at Bowden House

Ten minutes later, sipping black coffee in the courtyard outside, Marion ditched all of my notions of travelling through time, pointing out that the séance had created a psychic window allowing us to peek into another realm of reality, a place where time has no meaning and lost lives remain in perpetual stability. I preferred the theory of a subconscious daydream to a time-slip or trip to another realm, but on reflection I believe my doubts back then to be a natural reaction to an occurrence I could not understand.

The sadness and empathy I had felt for a Tudor lady lost somewhere between dimensions lingered around me for days afterwards, raising the question once again: was she real or fantasy? Either way, Marion released her the next morning.

Me, a medium?

I had been told by three individual mediums that I had the gift, so armed with a little bit of knowledge I jumped in. I failed to take note of my instincts telling me that another learning curve lay ahead and for a while my fascination with what I found I could pick up when I opened my psyche very soon turned to desperation, as the realisation hit me that I had absolutely no idea how to switch it off.

Turning to Marion for help, I received a rather harrowing ticking off regarding my lack of self-discipline. The emotional and psychological pressures I had to endure as my reasoning with logic and belief became stretched to the limit are far too complex and personal for inclusion here, and would be better suited to a future book. However, this was the most extraordinary part of my life as an investigator of the paranormal, and although I later turned away from the mediumistic path, I found that I had attained a new addition to the ghost hunter's kitbag, a very special tool that has never let me down.

The
Lost
Ones

Cellars are not the most comfortable of places to spend the night. Dark, musty and cold, it came as no great surprise that the staff of the White Hart Hotel in St Albans felt the cellar at their premises to be haunted. The atmosphere in the hotel's lower depths was nothing short of horrible, a feeling so embracing that it was a challenge for anybody to remain down there for long periods.

Rebecca

Most hauntings have a traceable pattern, such as a particular room, a doorway or a corner where even the most sceptical individual would admit to feeling different or odd. But in this particular cellar, it wasn't just the walls or the doorway that were frightening, it was the entire space. Every brick, every corner, each held an aura of irrational dread. Something awful had happened here, a tragedy so terrifying that the imprint left behind remained locked in a pitiful state of despair, forever present, forever dominating.

Over the years, I have investigated countless haunted houses and come across heartbreaking tales of tragedy and murder, but it was here that one of the saddest tales of my career was to unfold. The baseline tests revealed a number of temperature fluctuations and some unusual electromagnetic readings, but nothing that immense to indicate any sign of strong activity. In fact, no paranormal phenomena had been reported from the cellar, only a feeling, a feeling of wanting to get out.

Other than a few ghost stories, the team and I knew nothing of the White Hart's history upon arrival, so uniquely we were all in the dark regarding the facts on this occasion. As we entered the cellar for the first time, accompanied by a researcher and two other mediums, Joy Henson and Paul Hanrahan, Marion immediately began to pace the room attempting to tune into the energy to locate the cause and sure enough, curled up in one of the musty corners hiding, she soon found the ghost of a terrified little girl.

She guessed that the child was aged between four and six years old, and, from the way she was dressed, hailed from the 18th century. She was so frightened that it took all Marion's parental skills to coax the little girl into even acknowledging her presence. When finding the lost souls of children, the natural reaction is to perform a rescue as quickly as possible, but for us to do this we first had to discover her background before any reasonable attempt could be made to release her trapped spirit from its earthbound torment.

The three mediums arranged themselves into a semicircle, closing their eyes in concentration as the process of opening up began. After limited success with a routine linking exercise, Marion decided that the only way to proceed was by conducting a trance mediumship session, a method where the subject puts aside all of her sensory boundaries and invites the spirit in temporarily to take over part of the body, thus allowing the lost soul to speak.

Rational and calm, Marion prepared herself, throwing me a comforting smile before closing her eyes to commence her trance. Fifteen minutes had passed by in silence before I suddenly noticed that the room was growing increasingly cold. Joy and Paul were already aware of the change in atmosphere and once the time was right, the questions began.

Andy in the White Hart's cellar

'Is there somebody here that needs our help?' whispered Joy. 'We are not going to hurt you. We mean you no harm. We are simply here to help.'

A spine-tingling scream screeched from Marion's mouth as the spirit of the child connected, finding voice for the first time in countless years. She was hysterically screaming for her mummy to let her out, to come and get her. I was numb with shock, for although I had seen Marion trance many times before I had never been witness to a display such as this. In the space of a second, Marion's gentle character had changed from a sleep-like slumber to a now screaming child, wet with tears, red in the face, her nose dribbling with mucus. The screams were so intense that it took Joy at least five minutes to be heard over the heartbreaking agony emanating from the medium's mouth as she flinched and shook in her chair.

The very thought that this was a child brought tears to my eyes. The helplessness I felt, the natural reaction to reach out and comfort her was overwhelming, but impossible to act upon. For over 45 minutes Joy persisted in vain to try and calm the spirit, until eventually, sapped of energy, the child went limp and both mediums finally managed to reach her.

With the child now still inhabiting Marion but devoid of the strength to move away, it was time for her to be released from the last moments of life that she had been clinging on to for over 200 years. Her little bubble of timeless unreality created by her own fear had been burst, enabling the dense atmosphere inhabiting the cellar slowly to disperse. As a witness, the scene now resembled one of a child being slowly rocked to sleep. Comforted by Joy, the last word the ghost whispered before she left was her name: Rebecca.

All that remained was for the mediums to bring forward a spiritual guide to collect the little girl and hopefully reunite her with her family.

Conclusion

The historical records in the St Albans library read that in 1803 a fire had raged through the White Hart claiming the life of a five-year-old girl who had been locked in the cellar earlier that day as a punishment for being naughty. As the fire took a hold, the crowd that gathered around the girl's mother could do nothing but watch the inferno engulf the building.

The evening had been upsetting for all involved, especially Marion, who found it difficult to distance herself from the experience. For some time afterwards, she retained a continual concern for the little girl, wondering if she had indeed found peace following her release.

Three years later in Cyprus, Marion was approached by a woman, a stranger claiming to be a medium, who told her that she had a message from a little girl called Rebecca. The message simply said, 'Thank you, Marion. I'm living with the angels now.'

The lost ones

Many ghosts, especially children, are left behind purely due to their innocence and inability to acknowledge or understand death. Why some remain while others go smoothly on is questionable, but if a person unexpectedly dies instantly under tragic circumstances, the initial shock of detachment from the physical body is so quick that for a while they can believe themselves to be still alive.

There are many instances connected to this theory found in numerous haunted house reports where the ghost simply carries on with his or her daily routine completely unaware of his or her physical state. Some remain stuck in time, repeating their final moments before death over and over until eventually, after many years, the building holding them is radically changed or demolished. With nothing left to hold them, the haunting ceases and the surviving energy releases itself.

Another more slightly humorous reason for a haunting is the tangled web of affection felt by one or more people in life that carries on after death, which can cause spirits to trap themselves. I came across such a case at a hotel in Rumney, South Wales in January 2007. The top floor of this building that once served as an orphanage is not the kind of place I would recommend for somebody sensitive to this type of phenomenon to take up residence.

Within the space of an hour of our arrival, two guest investigators broke down in tears, claiming they were fearful of an evil presence, while another sensed that children had been subjected to abuse. The orphanage suffered greatly with many children dying following an outbreak of tuberculosis that ravaged southern Wales in the 1800s. It soon became evident that this was no ordinary haunting, for the building appeared to be absent of any interactive entities. However, the residual energy of those awful events that occurred years ago was very much still a fabric of the building, infesting every door, stair, room and walkway. Many people having spent a short period of time alone on the top floor reported seeing clear visions of the past that would flit across the mind, providing a pictorial insight into the building's history.

Despite all the hardship, there was one woman who watched over the orphans and as she lay on her deathbed, struck down by infection, she refused to leave the children even in death. As each child died, she held them close to her, protecting them, completely unaware that her actions were preventing any of her flock from leaving. The situation had developed into a stalemate with a connected collection of energies all bonded by love refusing to let go of one another.

The atmosphere was sickly and the solution was obvious. The key to all of this was to release the spirit of the nanny so that the children would follow. However, the strength of the bond was virtually unbreakable and far too complex for one single medium to achieve.

Reluctantly we had no choice but to leave them where they were in the hope that some day nature would eventually embrace what was lost.

Upon my return home I felt sick and utterly depressed and after three days my fear of a possible spirit attachment from the place began to grow. I felt no presence of a ghost, but the overwhelming desire for human comfort and reassurance led me to believe that perhaps some part of the hotel had come home with me. Thankfully this condition, diagnosed as a psychic hangover, lasted for only six days and I later discovered that, with the exception of Marion, the entire team had suffered from it.

Midnight playtime

On a lighter note, children in spirit can be just as playful as they were in life. During the investigation of a wandering monk near a castle in Cornwall one year, I traced the path allegedly walked by the ghost across the grounds, through a hedge and down a country lane until finally the line came to an end by a row of cottages. Knocking from door to door, the owners were all keen to tell their own stories of the legends associated with the local castle and the ghosts that apparently haunt it, but one couple in particular had a very personal story to tell.

Some years ago they had lost a five-year-old son to an illness, but they were convinced that the boy was still with them. Having an hour or so to spare, I agreed to listen to their story. My immediate reaction was pity, for to lose a child is any parent's nightmare. But I remained open minded whilst at the same time grounded, for wishful thinking can create a false scenario for anybody experiencing grief at this level.

Following the funeral, the child's clothes and toys had been locked away by the parents, who were too distraught to part with them. Exactly one year to the day after his death, the father came down one morning to ready himself for work and discovered his son's toys spread all over the lounge floor. Believing this to be the work of his wife who had perhaps woken in the night, desperate for a connection with her lost son, he called her down only to find that she was just as bemused as he was.

Picking them up one by one, they began to reminisce and for the first time in over a year, finally talk about their son's short life and the memories they shared. Rather confused with the occurrence they dutifully packed the toys away, only to discover them all the next morning, littered once again about the front room. Both parents had never had any real interest in the paranormal but felt sure that this had to be their son returning home from heaven to let them know he was okay.

The incident with the toys went on for a week until one night the couple bedded down for the night in the lounge, hoping that they may see him one more time. In a dream that night, the boy came to his mother to say goodbye. When she asked him why he had to go, the boy replied that playtime was over and he wouldn't be able to come back again. She awoke with a start to find her husband wide-eyed in disbelief. Both had dreamt the same dream at the same time and from then on, with a healthy slice of closure behind them, they began to live their lives once again.

The toys remained locked away. The midnight playtime was over.

The un-haunted house

Alas, not all haunted homes are what they appear to be. In 2004, a request from a family in Doncaster to investigate the haunting of their semidetached council house was brought to my attention by a friend of the family. On the face of it, the report read as a typical textbook-style haunting: objects vanishing and then reappearing around the house, crashes in the night and eggs found smashed.

The family of three consisted of two parents and the father's 13-year-old girl daughter from a previous marriage. The opinion was that a poltergeist was focusing in on the child. However, around

4am having set up a locked-off hidden camera, the girl was filmed on the stairway throwing objects down the wooden stairs and after a little heart-to-heart the next morning, the missing articles were found under her bed.

Conclusion: a simple case of an attention-seeking child.

Northern Ireland's Greatest Haunts

From the very start I was adamant that *Greatest Haunts* was not going to be just another ghost-hunting TV series shot in night vision. I wanted something different. Before writing the format, I viewed many of the shows circulating the networks, including the ones I had worked on in the past, and decided it was time for something fresh and new.

With this new series, my initial aim was to return to the kind of honesty that was present during the filming of *Ghost Detectives* in 2001, a series that came out a full year before *Most Haunted*, only this time mix it with a lot more analysis and history. Furthermore, I was determined that the paranormal investigations within the series were to be conducted correctly and, to the best of our resources, scientifically and that all 'evidence' would be open to debate.

The feeling from many people I spoke to at the time was that enthusiasts working in this field of study were sick and tired of the

Andy, Jane Wardrop (left) and Michelle O'Dowd

usual humdrum nonsense continually being churned out on TV, and viewers were longing to see the work of a paranormal investigator being portrayed from a different perspective that acknowledged it as a serious subject. However, the development of my new series was not without setbacks.

In the meantime, I joined *Haunted Homes* for the last three episodes of series two, but the show didn't continue. On the brighter side, while lecturing for the Zoological Society of London (ZSL), I scribbled a few ideas on a scrap of paper. The final draft for *Haunted Ireland* (working title) was written two weeks later in the back of a car as Marion and I headed down to Southampton on a theatre tour.

Over to Ireland

I have always had a fondness for Ireland and am constantly asked why I gave my three children, Aiden, Liam and Daniel, Irish names. It never occurred to me as to why until 2007 when it came to light whilst researching our family history that my great-great-great-grandfather was an Irishman called Richard, which as it happens is my middle name. Not a lot can be told about him since the records in Dublin were destroyed in a fire many years ago, but I like to think that perhaps my ancestral route back to Ireland with the TV series was more than just a coincidence. Perhaps a little outlandish, perhaps not, but my instincts when I am over there tell me above all else that I have come home.

In June 2007, I opted to bypass UK broadcasters with the idea simply because at the time the market was still awash with paranormal 'entertainment' series. For a country knee-deep in myth and legend, I was amazed to discover that Ireland had never had its own series based on the subject. Linda Cullen, head of TV at Coco Television, jumped at it and before long I found myself on a plane bound for Belfast to pitch the idea to the commissioning editors at BBC Northern Ireland. In late October, following two more meetings, the call came that six episodes had been commissioned.

At this stage the series was still entitled *Haunted Ireland*. Together with Coco TV and the BBC, we crafted a series that not only looked great, but was also rich in history and studied all the myths surrounding hauntings whilst covering the mediumistic and scientific aspects of the paranormal in an optimistic way. To our delight, the show became a massive hit in Ireland.

Marion Goodfellow

The original format included an Irish medium working with Marion, but the BBC was happy for her to work on her own. As I have already explained, Marion has been a colleague and good friend of mine for many years. She excels at dealing with people from all walks of life, and regards her belief in the afterlife as factual knowledge rather than insight, a conviction that is matched only by her gift and honesty. In her own words, she repeatedly states that she is not out to provide proof to sceptics, for proof is something only an individual can decide upon once the evidence has been placed on the table.

The investigation team

When picking a team for the series I looked at many different options. To start with, I knew many great groups in the UK, but felt that if I was to move forward then I needed to start afresh and leave the past behind. There are some great groups in Ireland and after spending two days sifting through the internet, the Northern Ireland Paranormal Society was in my sights.

What struck me straight away about the people in this society was their knowledge and scientific, open-minded devotion to studying this type of phenomenon, and although they had a limited amount of media experience, I was amazed at their natural ability in front of camera when we came to film episode one. The team had taken part in a BBC radio series with Gerry Anderson some years before, and luckily all of them had the right personalities to make a

TV series without any egotistical nonsense rearing its head. Darren Ansel, Tony Armstrong, Mark Cowden, Roddy and Raymond Breslin and Julia Irvine are a very close-knit team and in many ways remind me of the bond I shared with *Ghost Detectives*.

The Northern Ireland Paranormal Society

Irish folklore and legend

Perhaps more than any other country in the world, Ireland is revered for its mythical and legendary tales that have been handed down from generation to generation for the past 2,000 years. Even now in the 21st century, the folklore that originated from those early Druid stories is still prominent in rural areas right across the four provinces. Sit yourself down in any village pub and you will find legendary tales of banshees and little people spun by characters as timeless as the tales they tell. It is a great shame that these wonderful storytellers are perhaps a dying breed, because as we head further into this new millennium, technology seems far more appealing to the young than hearing yet another of great-granddad's superstitious yarns. As a result, the grand old book of folklore may be in danger of ending up forgotten on some dusty shelf.

Not too long ago, fairies were believed to have dwelled under mounds of earth and were reputed to bring misfortune to anybody who dared touch them. Children of a bygone age would search the forest trees for a leprechaun in the hope that, once caught, he would lead them to a pot of gold. However, the legends say that if you take your eyes off him just once, both leprechaun and gold vanish before your very eyes.

All fanciful stuff, but it is relevant to note that nearly all famous legends, such as King Arthur and Robin Hood, have a historical element of truth. Who is to say that perhaps back in Ireland's distant past a villager once came across a dwarf traveller who, agreeing to trade possessions with him, tricked the villager with the promise of a bag of gold. Gathering up the man's food and blanket, the dwarf headed off into the forest to collect the gold but never returned to pay for his goods. Legends and myths are stories handed down and each time tales such as these are told and then retold over the years, facts soon become fiction until one day all that remains of the simple story of the dishonest dwarf is an entertaining tale of leprechauns.

Some legends transcend the warm log fire or bedtime tale and offer a more tangible slice of reality. The Blarney Stone is perhaps a good example, for it is said that if you kiss this age-old stone then you will be granted the gift of fluent speech, what some call the gift of the gab. It is one half of a magical stone called the Stone of Scone and such was the belief that it held special powers that many Scottish kings were crowned over it.

In 1314, the stone was given to Cormac Teige McCarthy by Robert the Bruce as a gift for his assistance in the battle of Bannockburn, and soon after it was placed high up in the battlements of Blarney Castle. The story goes that Cormac, Lord of Blarney, kissed the stone and was subsequently cured of his speech impediment. At this point in history, Queen Elizabeth I wished to occupy Irish chieftain lands and claim them for the Crown. Cormac, having pronounced his loyalty to Elizabeth, somehow won over the Queen with his sweet-talking diplomacy and persuaded her not to take control of his land, upon which she amusingly stated that Cormac was talking a lot of blarney, hence the legend.

Such is the power of tradition that even today people travel from far and wide to kiss this mystical stone. In fact Ireland's legends and superstitions are so revered that the emblem of the land, the shamrock, once proclaimed by St Patrick as an example of the proof of the Holy Trinity, is worn with pride by millions worldwide.

Of all the mythical tales associated with Ireland, the one that interests me above all is the legend of the banshee. This female ancestral spirit is rarely seen, but often heard wailing her forewarning of an impending death. Legend has it that only five Gaelic families are able to hear her: the O'Gradys, the O'Neills, the O'Briens, the O'Connors and the Kavanaghs. According to those who claim to have seen her, the image of the banshee takes on three different forms: a young girl; a stern-looking matron; and a rather disturbing witch-like old hag. The banshee has perhaps transcended the folklore tradition, as many people in Ireland today still claim to hear her wailing, piercing cry on the eve of a family member's death.

The reports come from a wide cross-section of people from the cities as well as the more rural areas, and whilst researching locations for the TV series I was very surprised at the belief held in the legend of the banshee by the Irish population.

This particular folklore has many similarities to what parapsychologists call a crisis apparition, a unique type of ghost that to my knowledge is one of the most commonly reported by people from all cultures and walks of life. At the point of death, the spirit of a brother, sister or relative – in this case let's call him Uncle Jack – will appear to a living family member not as a spectral transparent image as one would think, but as a solid-looking, living person. Uncle Jack says his goodbyes and then vanishes. All becomes apparent to the bemused relative when news comes through that dear old Uncle Jack passed away in hospital at the exact time he appeared to bid farewell. Many believe that banshees are nothing but shadows, floating amongst our realm feeding upon human grief to sustain their power.

The classic depiction of a banshee is the image of a tall, humanoid figure shrouded in a black cloak, under which no face can be seen except by one of the family of the soon-to-be deceased.

Armed with a little knowledge of the country's mythical past, I was set to explore the mysteries that lay buried deep in the heart of *Haunted Ireland*.

Armagh
Jail

I could smell the fear. The instinct to walk away, to avoid the murky depression infesting the atmosphere entrapped within the walls for countless years was almost overpowering. My emotions remained stable, in check, whilst my perception provided me with an insight into what lay ahead. Somewhere inside Armagh Jail was a brooding presence and whoever or whatever it was knew I was coming.

Constructed between 1780 and 1819 in two significant stages, Armagh Jail comprised three prisons, one for women, one for debtors and one for felons, as well as buildings for the block treadmill and engine house. Although the jail finally closed its doors in 1986, today it stands as a landmark in the town, overlooking a busy high street. Due for renovation, this would be the last chance to walk the original building before modern development stepped in and swept away much of its history.

Andy in Armagh Jail

Stories of ghosts are rife in the jail and even passers-by have stated that on occasions faces have been seen staring out of the long-empty windows. Council workers currently working on the site have all reported an immense sense of fear and trepidation within the building, so much so that even the tough, hardy builders refuse to walk the corridors alone.

Except that its residents lack their own key and room service, jails are similar to hotels, housing all manner of people from all walks of life. So with so many different emotions passing through the building over the years, it's hardly surprising that some residual memory of the inhabitants still remains locked within. The question is: did the jail really house ghosts, or are these reported experiences simply the result of an overactive imagination fuelled by the structure's history?

Standing in the main entrance hall, it isn't difficult to imagine what it must have been like to be marched through the main doors, stripped of your clothes, hosed down and then incarcerated in a tiny cell for 22 hours a day alongside petty thieves and murderers. Many never made it out alive, due to the cramped, insanitary conditions that created a breeding ground for diseases such as typhoid and cholera. The tough regime, harsh punishments and unhealthy conditions are well documented and stand today as a historical example of what life must have been like inside one of Northern Ireland's infamous old jails.

There are many different reasons why a particular building or place could be haunted. It could be that someone just doesn't want to move on after death and so chooses to remain at home in surroundings he or she recognises and trusts. Others can pass so suddenly that they are blissfully unaware that they have, in fact, died. In these cases, their consciousness creates the illusion that the world around them is normal, so they carry on with their daily routine completely oblivious to their non-physical state.

What does interest me is that many reported ghosts seem to date from the 15th to 19th centuries. You never hear of Neolithic cave man ghosts wandering around haunted sites, and I think this has to do with religious belief. Not so long ago, if you stole an apple you could be hanged and damned to spend eternity in hell for your crime. At the point of death with the fear of damnation staring you in the face on your judgement day, ask yourself what you would do: go forward into the light facing God's wrath and eventual imprisonment in hell as the society of the time has taught you, or save yourself and remain where you are as a ghost lost between worlds, too fearful to move on?

Daniel

It was mid-morning, the air was crisp for late August and as I made my way into the building I was met by Trevor Geary from Armagh District Council, who proceeded to show me around the now derelict governor's quarters and the cells that once housed the criminally insane deep underground. The tour was for my benefit, because Trevor could pinpoint specific areas where witnesses had claimed to have experienced ghostly encounters.

Despite my expectations, I personally felt nothing to indicate a haunting apart from some vague sense of a janitor-like presence walking around the walkway on the second floor of the women's wing. This presence certainly wasn't aware of me and, rather than a conscious spirit, was probably a residual memory trace that would most likely be extinguished should the site ever be demolished. However, my enthusiasm was heightened when I began to dowse the first cell block, accurately pinpointing the condemned cell and the unmarked grave of Joseph Fee, the last man to be hanged at Armagh for murder in 1904.

So far the walk-around with Trevor had been a pleasant morning, but as I headed towards A Wing, the men's wing, the atmosphere changed, as from within I sensed a powerful force barring my way.

The electromagnetic field was so dense and heavy that anybody with even the slightest psychic ability would feel dizzy and drained having once walked through it. Once again, my instincts appeared to be accurate, as Trevor stated that this particular area is where few favour to walk alone.

As I moved forward I felt protected within myself but remained on guard, for although I could physically walk into A Wing, the dowsing rods remained static, indicating that I had no permission to enter from whatever resided within.

The musty, damp smell of decay hung in the air like some dreadful perfume. With every step forward, the eerie sensation of being watched from each cell doorway was highlighted by shadows dancing in unison with the reflections of sunlight emanating from the sunbathed, shrine-like windows located at the far end of the

The haunted A Wing at Armagh Jail

corridor. I immediately understood the builders' apprehension of walking the vast corridor of cells alone, for in here of all places, one would never be alone. Furthermore, whoever was generating these negative sensations was angry, very angry.

About halfway into the wing, the heavy, dizzy atmosphere lifted and I stopped, confused and intrigued by its sudden disappearance. Cautiously retracing my steps, the awful feelings began to return, steadily at first then increasing like some gloomy blanket creeping up my body. The wing appeared to have two energy fields, one negative, the other positive, and I guessed that whatever entity inhabited the area could not move from one to the other. Why these vastly different cocoons of energy were here was anybody's guess. My evaluation at the time was that the anger and frustration exuded over many years by the ghost had virtually transmitted his surviving energy into the walls, the floors, even the doors, until ultimately he had literally become part of the physical surroundings.

Checking out my theory, I moved two steps forward once again and sure enough the feelings were gone in an instant, replaced by a lighter vibe that was equal to the pleasure of taking in a breath of fresh sea air. It was as if I had walked through a doorway into a new room and surprisingly my dowsing rods were now working perfectly, giving me positive readings regarding permission, protection, in fact answers to any questions I cared to ask. Bearing this in mind I decided now was the time to attempt contact.

'Is there anybody there?' The question is an obvious one to ask and I prefer to use the term 'anybody' as opposed to calling out for astral beings, spirit people or other such outlandish titles that in my opinion simply confuse and depersonalise communication.

Before I had even finished asking the question, the rods jerked into life and I felt a presence come forward, tentatively at first keeping some distance, but as the minutes passed whatever was there began to gain more confidence.

Using the yes/no dowsing technique, I was able to discover that the entity was a young man in his mid–20s serving three years in jail for a minor offence committed in 1896. He was calm, almost content to serve his time, whilst looking forward to a fresh start upon his release. Over the course of the next 10 minutes, I went through the alphabet, picking out possible names from each letter until finally the dowsing rods settled upon the letter D and moments later the name Daniel.

I asked Daniel if there were other inmates in the jail with him, to which he answered yes. Moving on, I suggested that he take a good look around him and think long and hard as to whether he thought he should still be here. This seemed to create a lot of confusion and I began to feel pity for this lad who, if my information was correct, had been stuck in a crumbling old jail for 112 years for a petty offence long since forgotten. I pondered upon my next decision. I couldn't leave him here, but without an experienced medium by my side the risk of what I was about to do was in my hands and should anything go wrong then it would be my responsibility alone.

I could still feel the lad's energy not far away from me and I wondered what he made of me. Was I real or was this a dream to him? Could he actually see me and if so did he, in turn, perceive me as a ghost?

The time for hesitation had passed. There was only one way to say this and I said it: 'Daniel, you don't belong here any more. You died a long time ago. You can leave. Let me help you.'

My heart began to beat faster and without any warning an overwhelming despair swept over me and within seconds I was on my knees sobbing, all the time wondering to myself what on earth was happening. The sheer grief and panic was immense and despite my physical state I realised that I had linked with the spirit of this lad. I was now feeling what he was feeling: shock, terror, panic, confusion, the disbelief that he was dead, that he would never see his family again.

It was as if I had awoken him from a dream. The world that he had created for himself was gone and now for the first time in over 100 years he could clearly see his surroundings: the decay, the emptiness of this place and the realisation that he had been dead for a long, long time.

I could feel him holding on to me, terrified and refusing to let go. Now in a blind panic myself, I shouted time and again for him to get back, but there seemed no way to break away. With such a strong grip on me I was fully aware that the entity was fast becoming a part of me and if I didn't act soon, this innocent act of salvation on my part could turn far more problematic for me to handle alone. I did what I could to separate the situation from my senses, quickly creating a psychic shield of protection around me that immediately broke the psychic link.

Free at last, I looked up and for a moment could see him backing away, head in hands, sobbing uncontrollably. He was so small, almost child-like in height. In the blink of an eye the image was gone, but the spirit remained, begging for help. I calmly promised him that help was on the way and that I would not abandon him.

I felt an arm help me to my feet and realised I had completely forgotten Trevor who had been observing the actions of the last 10 minutes. He seemed rather calm considering what had just happened and asked me if I was all right. As we left the wing, he noted that he felt calmness in himself now that somebody had made contact with one of the ghosts within, and sure enough, the atmosphere that had before been very heavy was now slightly relaxed.

Bring in the NIPS

Before we continued with anything, I opted to bring in the investigation team a little earlier than planned simply because, despite all that happened, I needed a second opinion of what we had already experienced. The Northern Ireland Paranormal Society, led by Darren Ansel and Tony Armstrong, conducted a series of tests later that night and found no unusual electromagnetic or infrasound readings to account for the experiences reported. (Infrasound is a bass wave vibration with a frequency below the audibility range of the human ear.) However, an unexplained low, cackling laugh was heard by three investigators on the second floor of the women's wing. Even more bizarrely, Tony Armstrong, a self-confessed sceptic, was clearly shaken during an electronic voice phenomena (EVP) experiment in the women's wing when a shadowy apparition was captured on the team's DV camera. If that wasn't enough, a hand

Monitoring possible activity

reached out and touched him, causing him to jump suddenly into the air.

To capture an apparition on film is very rare indeed, but to see it make a conscious move and physically touch somebody indicates an awareness that is rarely witnessed by more than one person at the same time. Later that afternoon, we gathered together in the control room to hear what our sound technician Mark had got so excited about just hours before. He explained that the audio we were about to hear was recorded the previous night up on the second floor of A Wing.

The first voice to be heard was plainly Tony's asking if there was anybody here that wanted to talk and if so were they imprisoned for a crime they didn't commit. The hiss of white noise echoed around our little room and was abruptly cut short by a male voice buried within the static asking with a pleading tone, 'Please help me...' My immediate thought was that this was the voice of Daniel somehow manipulating the static. Whatever the cause or origin was, somebody, somewhere was asking for help.

The rescue

I had a responsibility. I had made this spirit aware of his state and although this may have been a mistake, nevertheless I had made a promise. Help was indeed on the way in the form of my old friend and tutor, spiritualist medium Marion Goodfellow, who was due to arrive the following day with no prior knowledge of where she was going or what to expect.

Within seconds of entering the jail, Marion sensed a small, young man come towards her. The name she got from this entity was Daniel. I was dumbstruck, because as a psychic investigator I have to look for other logical explanations regarding hauntings; but since I had experienced this personally myself I found it difficult to even dare and try debunk what had happened.

When I finally met up with Marion later that afternoon, she had completed her assessment of the building. She had come across not only Daniel but also an altogether more aggressive character in A Wing by the name of Jack, who had continually taunted her with threats of murder and a promise that he would cut off certain parts of her body unless she left the jail immediately.

I requested that we conduct a rescue procedure for Daniel before we continue and at 5pm that afternoon we did just that. We opted to perform this clearing in the reception area by the main doors to A and B Wings. As we settled in, Marion performed a prayer of protection, not just for us, but also for the spirit she was to try and help move on.

Standing to her left side, I felt the temperature begin to rise, and recalling my encounter the previous day, I recognised the warmness of Daniel's presence. Marion instructed me to keep him close while

Rescuing Daniel (taken from the TV footage)

she connected with someone on the other side who could help, and eventually she stated that Daniel's mother was on her way. For somebody such as myself who 10 or so years ago scarcely believed in the existence of life after death or ghosts, I couldn't help but wonder for a moment how on earth I came to be here in a derelict Northern Ireland jail holding on to the ghost of a young man while we waited for the spirit of his mother to come and collect him.

Strange as it may seem, although very unscientific, this part of the job has always been fascinating. There was no blissful song of angels or heavenly lights when Daniel's mother arrived, just a pure feeling of joy accompanied by a pleasant, warm surge of electricity that passed through me as if in thanks. With mother and son reunited, we simply opened a doorway, an exit to this dimension, then stood back and allowed nature to take its course.

It was over within minutes, the spiral of emotion intense as relief and reconciliation paved the way for salvation. Daniel had no trouble leaving. He felt safe, he had his mother and, most important of all, he now had his freedom.

I have my own beliefs that are based upon personal experience and I keep these close to my heart, for although investigating claims of a haunting may in itself seem a little bizarre, taking part in a ceremony to clear a trapped soul is something altogether different. Some say that ghosts don't exist and that the unknown is best left alone, but what happened to me at Armagh Jail was real. I was there, I experienced it and if in any way we had helped a lost soul find his peace, then what could be so wrong about that?

The team's evaluation of their time spent in the jail proved to be a positive, as each member claimed to have felt, heard, sensed or seen something that could not be explained. With only one day left before we had to leave, this investigation had been short, so while Mark evaluated the film and audio footage, there was only one job left for us to complete.

The clearance

I was a little apprehensive. My concern for Marion's safety was paramount because I had made another promise a long time ago, not to a spirit but to her husband Ian, that I would never allow Marion to come to any harm or take unnecessary risks. Over the years, we have found ourselves in many a tight spot, but our bond of trust in one another has always guided and protected us both.

Making our way back into A Wing, I sensed something different. The atmosphere was the same, but the anger felt earlier had been replaced by another distinctive emotion: fear. Whatever part of Jack's life remained within this place was now afraid.

The team, comprising myself, Darren, Tony and Marion, settled into a circle of chairs laid out specially directly opposite cell 13,

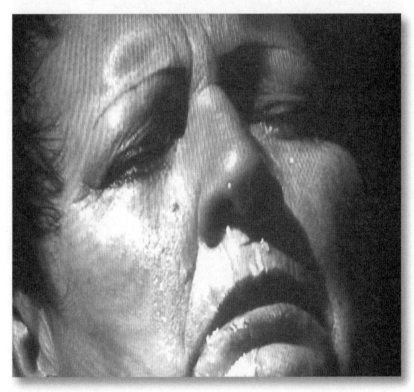

Marion channelling Jack at Armagh Jail (taken from TV footage)

smack in the middle of the men's wing and central to the area of ill feeling. Marion's aim was to attempt to contact the angry spirit causing all the oppression and somehow persuade it to let us help. The rescue we performed with Daniel was routine, but with this presence the procedure would require a certain amount of tact and patience. Marion decided to attempt contact through trance meditation. She already knew the name of the entity as Jack from her first encounter with him the day before, but to help him would involve her slipping into a self-hypnotic subconscious state somewhere between sleep and awake and inviting the spirit to connect and talk through her.

Marion channels the ghost of Jack (taken from the TV footage)

I have always been a little dubious with trance work, because the subconscious mind is so locked into a dream-like state that any information presenting itself is hardly useful as evidence. But the point of this exercise was to release the alleged entity, not prove its existence.

I counted Marion down from ten to one and when I was sure she was under, I began to ask if there was anybody there who wanted to come forward. As the time passed, Darren, Tony and I exchanged bemused glances, wondering if anything was going to happen at all. Suddenly, the temperature around us began to drop radically and the tortured voice of an irate Irish male screamed forth the words 'F*** off!' from Marion's doll-like mouth. The two lads were obviously shocked, as they knew Marion as a gentle lady of high standards, but I had witnessed this trance state many times before.

I decided to go for the direct approach, asking if the person present could give us his name. I received another disgruntled, 'F*** off,' only this time aimed directly at me.

Lightheartedly, I replied, 'So your name is F*** Off? My name is Andy and this is Tony and Darren. We are here to help you.'

'F*** off,' came the reply.

Darren butted in with a question: 'Jack, why are you so angry? Do you not want our help?'

No reply.

Gesturing to the surroundings with my hands, I offered this piece of logic to the ghost: 'Jack, this building won't be here much longer and we won't be coming back, so if you want us to help you leave this place then now is the time! You saw what we did with Daniel; we can help you in the same way.' Marion's face became contorted, her features began to tense. 'You don't belong here. Jack!' I continued. 'You've served your time.'

Marion's head turned towards Darren. 'F***ing royalist, are ya? My family was murdered by the bastards, all dead, dead! Do ya hear?' It appeared that we had hit a nerve and over the next 20 minutes the reason for the anger within this man became very understandable. Between us, we managed to bring out another side to the persona, a gentler, sorrowful victim of political circumstance.

We never found out why he had been imprisoned, but from the little information gleaned, we assumed that he was from around the late 1800s. For over an hour the team tried in vain to make him aware that he would not face damnation for his crimes, but his despair and fear were far too deeply embedded.

Taking the bull by the horns, I opened up and asked for help from the spirit guides that are said to sort out this kind of mess. Eventually, Jack's sister came through along with his mother and, despite a lot of tears, they took his hand and led him into the light.

When Marion came out of her trance she looked completely wrecked and retained no memory of the past hour-and-a-half. Darren and Tony, despite being enthralled by the whole experience, were unable to form any conclusive scientific thoughts.

There are many things in the world that we know little or nothing about and sometimes you have to reach out and grab the implausible, even when it is illogical. Where ancient man once threw rocks at the moon, he now has the ability to walk upon its surface and that's how I felt that afternoon, a tiny primitive speck in the universe reaching out in the darkness for help, to help another.

Throughout the four-day investigation of Armagh Jail, every piece of evidence – including names, dates and so on – were historically checked by our researchers. The name Daniel did crop up a number of times in the prison records for 1896, and indeed a young male prisoner was beaten to death in that year, but unfortunately without a surname no conclusive proof was evident. There were many encouraging prison records mentioning the name Jack, all convicted of a variety of crimes, but with no further information available we were unable to clarify if any of these may have been the entity we released.

Leaving the jail for the last time, I gazed back at the grim empty shell that once teemed with lost souls. I felt a warm glow in my heart for the victims of this place, trapped by their own human failings of a society long since past. But now they had been released and I found myself pondering an age-old question once again: what really happens when we die – where do we go? Had Jack and Daniel truly existed as we believed and, if so, were they both now at peace?

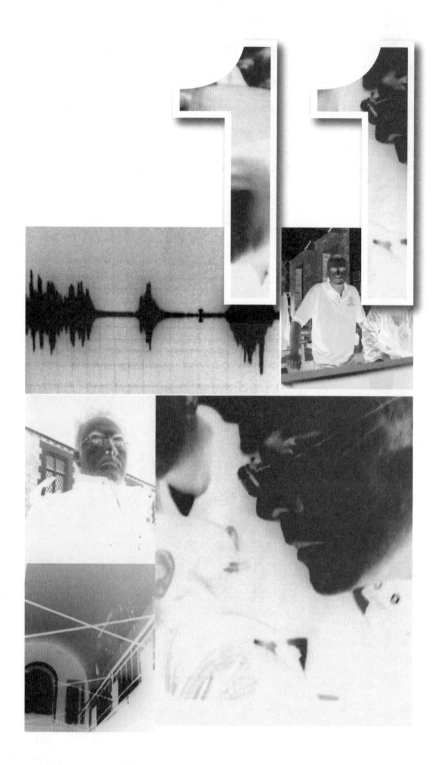

Wines and Spirits

'I can see water, a huge river with ships and dock workers right here where we are standing.' Marion's eyes gazed up and down the street as if searching for something lost long ago.

'My how this area has changed,' she whispered.

Direct Wine Shipments Warehouse, Belfast, September 2008

My view was somehow different. Cars parked, the old Presbyterian church over the road and the Direct Wine Shipments building behind me bore no resemblance to the images the medium was describing and why should it? This was the year 2008. But Marion's eyes told a different story, one that spoke of time being an illusion and I found myself wondering: was she really seeing the living past, Sailor Town, Belfast some 200 years ago?

Direct Wine is a thriving business run by two of the most honest, down-to-earth men you could ever wish to meet, namely Peter McAlindon and his younger brother Neal. The property is situated in one the oldest parts of Belfast on the edge of old Sailor Town and the cathedral quarter. Maps at the Harbour Commission show that the building was erected on the site of Ritchie's Dock between 1800 and 1820 on swampland landfill.

The early days of the building indicate that it was originally an entertainment tavern used by sailors and frequented by prostitutes. Throughout its life, the three-storey building has been home to a number of businesses, including a grain mill, a seed merchant, a whiskey distiller, a bakery, rope and canvas manufacturers, and a Kodak photography processing house, before finally becoming a wine warehouse in 1989.

Witness reports

Peter Gilfedder, a worker at the shop, was catching up on some work on a Sunday morning in the sales office on the third floor. Believing he was alone, Peter was surprised to come across a man sitting at the corner desk. Politely asking him who he was, Peter got the shock of his life when the man simply disappeared into thin air.

Ashen faced and visibly shaken, Peter made his way downstairs to report what he had seen. Both owners had frequently experienced uneasy feelings late at night when locking up, so were not surprised at their employee's story. Almost every night they felt that somebody was watching their every move, hurrying them along as if trying to force them out of the building.

Working alone one night on the top floor, Neal popped out to the staff kitchen for a coffee, but when he returned he found the chair he had been sitting on placed upside down on the floor. Neal is certain that if somebody had entered the building he would have seen or heard them come through the main door and climb the long, stone staircase.

The following week, an employee who, unbeknown to the brothers, had been stealing had a cup of coffee thrown at him from a seemingly unseen assailant. Once discovered, the employee was sacked, but this left the brothers in agreement that if there was indeed a ghost haunting the building, perhaps it was looking after their interests.

The story they had heard was that someone had committed suicide when the building was a photographic processing building. This was later backed up by a psychic lady who once sensed two spirits inhabiting the place, one of whom she felt had hanged himself.

On the day of my arrival, I felt nothing untoward in the building. All was calm, light and perfectly normal. I listened intently to the McAlindon brothers as they told me their stories of ghostly footsteps, voices and the dread felt by all on the top floor. At this point, I have to say that Peter and Neal are perfect category A witnesses. Both men are straight talkers, down-to-earth in attitude and basically a great couple of guys, certainly not the type to create a hoax or exaggerate.

Ghosts in the machine

An amateur musician, Peter frequently took advantage of the building's acoustics and on one dark, thundery night, having finished mixing tracks for a new song, he became aware of voices in the room with him. Tracing the source back to his amplifier, he assumed it was picking up a radio frequency, which is not uncommon.

But it was the content of the conversation emanating from the speaker that unnerved him. He could hear two people, a man and a woman, talking about what it's like to be dead, describing the normality of the afterlife as one would discuss the weather.

Quickly switching off the speakers, Peter made his way out on to the stairway and collected his coat, keys and additional work reports before hastily making his way down towards the first floor exit. Suddenly he stopped dead in his tracks, for from the room above he had just vacated the sound of loud heavy footsteps crossing from one side to the other began to reverberate down the long, dark corridor. Nervous and alone, Peter got out of the building as fast as he could.

Having heard their boss relay this story the next day, the staff were quick to admit that for some time they had all felt an overwhelming sensation of being watched from the stairway and felt afraid to venture there alone, although none of them could explain why. By day two I began to get a taste of what they meant.

Day two

I felt sick, giddy and off balance, symptoms usually associated with an ear infection or the onset of flu. Now with Marion on site, the unease within the place slowly escalated to a higher level of intensity. She had picked up the murder of a prostitute that had taken place on the second floor back in the days when the building was a tavern. Marion did what she had to do to help this woman, but with the poor woman's spirit trapped in a single moment in time it proved to be no easy matter.

From the woman's perspective, time had no meaning. In her reality, she was reliving her final seconds of physical life, curled up in the corner of the doorway dying from a stab wound, paralysed with fear. As we stood hand in hand around the centre of the energy, Marion's soft words of sympathy and understanding began to warm the atmosphere, indicating that a trust or temporary bond between the two had been accomplished.

Marion's experience as a medium was displayed to me once again as she tactfully avoided informing the woman that she was dead, for such a revelation would most certainly have caused the ghost to panic and we could have lost her for good. She explained that she was here to take her home, whispering that she had nothing to fear until eventually an understanding dawned and the dread that had once locked her in this timeless state subsided allowing nature to take its course. The first entity to haunt the warehouse had been released without any real fuss or effort.

More often than not, an investigator needs proof rather than the words of a medium, and science occasionally provides this. The team had set up an EVP experiment on the top floor wine tasting room and to assist them they had asked the owner's father to play the grand piano that stood in the corner. Since music is something we can all relate to, the theory was that maybe we could get some kind of reaction from other ghosts inhabiting the building by giving them something they could recognise.

Mr McAlindon senior played for 10 minutes, the keys and notes booming and bouncing from wall to wall in a manner that would literally wake the dead. As the final note resonated, the digital recording session began with a question asked by team leader Darren Ansel: 'If you enjoyed the lovely music, then let us know and we can play some more.' Not a word or a sound was heard by anybody present as we all stood not daring to breath until the sign was given that the experiment was over.

Our sound technician Mark Cowden had soon analysed the recording. On the playback the last notes of the piano gave way to silence that was cut short moments later by Darren asking his question. Logically, the remainder of the recording should have been clear since nothing was heard at the time, but a deep, resonating knock leapt out of the speakers. If this wasn't enough, a male voice then produced a slow spooky message. 'Will you – let her?' We played it over and over, but it made no sense in context to the question Darren had asked. Neither did the second voice that appeared to be French: 'Ici to va,' which at the time we translated to mean, 'Here to go'.

Listening to the French EVPs at Direct Wine

We were aware from my historical research conducted earlier that day that French sailors would have frequented the building in the 18th century. But, excited as we all were at this astonishing result, the words were far too random to be filed as a plausible intelligent response.

Mysteriously, as Mark continued to analyse the EVP, it emerged that the voice pattern wavefile matched our own, indicating that the French speech was, in fact, human, but nobody other than Darren had spoken and the playback from the video proved this beyond any doubt. Once we had ruled out any local shortwave radio emissions, such as taxis, the big question still remained: where on earth did it come from – another dimension?

A multidimensional universe

Many scientists believe that we live in a multidimensional universe. If this is true, then alternate realities should in effect co-exist alongside our own. Imagine a whole civilisation spanning various different points in time all living in their own individual reality right beside us but completely unaware of our existence.

Because we are all naturally conditioned not to see beyond what our senses allow us to, the whole concept sounds absurd; but perhaps under certain environmental conditions both sound and light operating on different frequencies within each dimension can somehow interact, creating a window that allows us to take a brief glimpse beyond our reality. This could be why so many people claim to see ghosts in places not reputed to be haunted. Furthermore, if this theory works both ways, perhaps we are appearing as ghosts in some other dimension right now.

Maybe death isn't a heaven or hell route after all. Once free of our bodily form, is it possible that our consciousness has the natural ability to transcend the boundaries surrounding us in life, thus allowing us to cross dimensions to begin a new existence in another?

Day three

Lunch hour on day three had been a strange affair. The food was great, as was the company, but the choice of dining area was beginning to attract something so sad that halfway through I simply had to leave the room to compose myself. One look from Marion said it all; this was not imagination, nor was it the effects of infrasound, which had been checked due to the location of the building standing near to a busy slip road. Even carbon monoxide levels were thoroughly checked beforehand, so why I felt so rough on the top floor of the building, yet felt fine elsewhere was a complete mystery.

The entity we both sensed was so strongly depressed that for brief moments I began to experience fleeting moments of panic. Sweating hands and palpitations, coupled with a strong desire to get out of there, exceeded my usual degree of healthy curiosity and I had to leave the building, close myself down, and shield myself emotionally and psychically in preparation for my return. As to who or what was the cause, I simply didn't care at the time.

The epicentre of the haunting at Direct Wine was not hard to find and curiously enough the location matched perfectly with past witness reports that stated an unknown source of fear that would suddenly take a hold should anybody enter.

Walking past the spot where Neal had discovered the upturned chair, we made our way into the back storeroom on the top floor. Before Marion had even stepped forward, she stated ominously that somebody had hanged themselves here. Macabre as this was, the story then became much darker as Marion explained that the unfortunate man had not died alone. People had watched, daring him to go through with it.

The spirit was essentially harmless, but, as with the young woman in the doorway, trapped nonetheless and in need of help. I began by introducing us both and offering a hand of help.

'"Jamie, me Jamie." That's what he's telling me.' Looking up at Marion I could see the complex confusion that mirrored the entity's persona as she searched for any information that could be gleaned from the ghost. 'He's praying,' she said.

Now was the time to act, but before we had the chance to channel him, the whole room changed. The atmosphere brightened and the depression lifted like a blanket suddenly ripped from a bed. Jamie, if that was his name, had fled.

Marion was adamant that he hadn't left the building, but the dismal notion that we had failed became ever more likely as I watched the medium go gently from one room to another, quietly searching for some sign of the lost soul hiding away. It seemed that on this occasion we were left with no choice but to leave this one to his own fate.

With the team now packing away, this investigation was drawing to a close. I was thankful for the evidence of the EVP, which obviously required further analysis, but couldn't hide the disappointment of leaving unfinished business behind. We had freed one lost woman in distress and it was now time to move on and focus upon the next location.

With lunchtime long since over, the small staff kitchen was empty, but the smell of soups, pasties and coffee remained, a ghostly

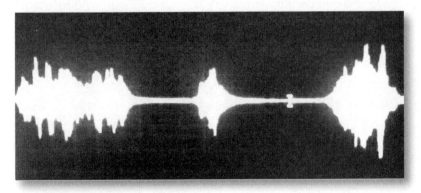

Wave file for analysing EVPs

reminder that imprints are always left behind. Clicking on the kettle, an immense wave of sadness and depression came back at me from where it was lurking near the far wall. Carefully checking the room space, mapping exactly where the intensity of the energy was located, I quietly retraced my steps back out on to the landing, motioning to Marion with a soft whistle to join me.

The medium worked fast, first drawing the energy towards her and then desperately holding on to the link, opening up a door to freedom that Jamie had long since been locked behind. She showed him his home, his front door with the number 12 where his family awaited his return within.

The comfort and belonging that the spirit so longed for was presented before him. With all thoughts of his entrapment momentarily extinguished, the tortured soul of Jamie was free, snapped instantly from a reality no longer relevant to him to a new plane where hopefully his existence would continue on in peace.

Conclusion

As I left Belfast, a thought struck me. The French EVP, 'Ici to va', which read in English 'Here to go', was perhaps not as irrelevant as first assumed. We had been 'here' in the building and had helped 'to' or 'two' go. Could this possibly have been a message from another spirit requesting we help two of Direct Wines ghosts move on?

On the other hand, with EVPs it is very difficult to understand clearly what is being said. The voice could have been saying, 'Ici tu va', which translates as 'Here you go'. Maybe when asked by Darren to leave us a message, some ghost inhabiting the building decided to give us some proof: 'Here you go, mate!'.

Coincidence or not, our job was finished.

The Butler Didn't Do It

I love the ocean. There's something about the sea that summons up a romantic fascination with time, for as you view each breaking wave, you are witness to an event once seen through the eyes of ancient peoples. Like the moon that forever orbits the earth, both have remained unchanged for millions of years, overseeing such events as the destruction of the dinosaurs, the construction of the great pyramids, endless wars and our first step into space.

Walking with historian Bob Pue along the seashore opposite Woburn House, the same could be said of the view spread out before me in this small corner of Northern Ireland known as Millisle. The picture in my possession was of an early 19th-century postcard depicting the grand building, now supposedly haunted, standing proud in its full glory, photographed over 80 years before from the exact position where I now stood.

Bob had worked at Woburn for over 30 years. With the rain beating down I listened as he relayed the legend of Woburn House. The ghosts, the murder of a pregnant servant girl by her lover, allegedly Woburn's butler, and his subsequent suicide all made the entire case sound like a murder mystery weekend.

Andy with Bob Pue

The butler, named Barkley, was said to have carried the girl's body to a line of rocks, now known as Barkley's Rock to the locals, where he dumped her into the sea. Later, ridden with guilt, he took a rope up to the tower house, which is now Bob's office, and hanged himself. A sad tale of uncontrolled passion, embellished through the years by local chat, had evolved into legend, leaving the name Barkley forever footmarked in Millisle's history and his ghost to wander the corridors of Woburn House.

This beautiful Georgian mansion house was originally home to John Gilmore Dunbar Esq. in 1824 and remained in the Dunbar family until the early 1900s, before finally passing to the Beresford family in 1934. Now home to the Northern Ireland Prison Service College, Woburn House also served its time as a borstal in the 1970s where my guide for the day had once worked as a prison officer. Bob's historical knowledge of the house was impressive and his passion for the prison service was evident in the splendour of the museum room that he alone had conceived and maintained for many years.

Woburn House, Millisle, in the early 1900s

Physical signs of a haunting generally range from strange odours, electrical problems and mild poltergeist activity through to ghostly whispers and manifestations. It's very rare that one comes across an energy so strong that it can psychically touch or attack a living person, but having listened to the testimony of Bob Pue, it appeared that Woburn could well be one of those rare cases.

Terror in the tower

Bob's office is located high up in the tower, a room prison guards used during the borstal years as a night-guard lookout point. The room itself was cosy, small and welcoming, harbouring no trace of the tragic demise of the butler all those years ago.

It had been a warm summer evening when Bob settled himself down for his night-guard shift. With the kettle on the boil, he stretched, laying out his feet to rest on the table, when all of a sudden the room turned strangely cold. As he made a move towards the radiator, unseen arms grabbed him from behind, holding him fast in a strong firm grip. Believing this to be one of his colleagues having a game, he jokingly shouted, 'Get off,' but his amusement quickly caved into fear as the reflection in the window ahead clearly showed that nobody was there.

For what seemed an eternity, Bob wrestled back and forth in his chair drawing on all of his strength in a pitiful attempt to free himself, but then events took an even more sinister turn as his cries for help became silenced by an invisible hand that became clasped over his mouth.

Fearful for his life, Bob persisted in his struggle, finally managing to remove his feet from the table before crashing to his knees on the office floor. The temperature within the room began to return to normal and with it, Bob's freedom of movement. Shaking with exhaustion and fear, he stood up, surveying the empty room and searching for some explanation of what had happened and the whereabouts of his attacker. Nobody was there. He was alone.

Bob's only conclusion was that he himself had encountered one of Woburn's lingering ghosts.

Weighing up Bob's story, I privately considered all the alternative explanations. If he had unknowingly dozed off in his chair this could have induced a kind of sleep paralysis episode where the body is naturally paralysed somewhere between wakefulness and sleep. On the rare occasions this happens it can be extremely frightening to an individual, because the experience is often accompanied by the sense of an evil presence lurking nearby. On a rather more worrying note, perhaps he had suffered a minor stroke, in which case a trip to the doctors would be advisable.

Behind the scenes at Woburn House

Bob dismissed both alternatives, convinced that what happened to him was real. Some weeks after his experience, another member of staff on duty in the watchtower was attacked in exactly the same way, but unlike Bob, this employee hurriedly handed in his resignation, never to return. With a few hours to spare I opted to take my own place in the office chair, but disappointingly spent the whole afternoon gazing out at the coastline through the window rather than encountering any poltergeists.

The flying pen

The prison officer training classroom room was like any other, with row upon row of tables each occupied by a PC and containing that underlying odour of human sweat that is unavoidable when large groups of people spend a few hours in such close quarters. Bob and I, accompanied by Jane Wardrop, Production Manager for Coco Television, now stood in the very room that had once served as a dormitory for young offenders. Her reason for coming along was to try and pinpoint locations and specific stories to include in the half-hour episode due to be filmed.

Although at the beginning of the series Jane admitted to having an interest in the paranormal, she never thought for one moment that she would encounter anything until nature called at Woburn House. Speaking in June 2009, she recalled her experience:

'My one prominent memory from the *Greatest Haunts* series was in Woburn House. It was about 7pm and the plan for the night was to set up a "ghost nest", a cluster of controlled object tests in an area where most activity had been reported. I went to the toilet and for the first time that day none of the crew were around or near the vicinity of the toilet. As I entered the toilet, I felt a little strange. It was as if I felt the presence of a woman in the loo. She followed me everywhere - from inside the cubicle to the sinks and to the hand dryer. But once I left the room, I felt nothing, which I thought strange. I ran out and told everyone that I had "felt a woman in the loo!", to which the crew started laughing and telling me, 'Well done!" Dirty minds! I still believe to this day that I was not alone in that toilet in Woburn.'

Standing near to the door all three of us were involved in deep conversation, thrashing out Millisle's history, its connection to the house, witnesses who were willing to be filmed and so on, when without warning, a red marker pen flew across the room, ricocheting off a PC before coming to rest with a soft clatter on the table before us.

One hand placed over her mouth, Jane, obviously alarmed, began to edge backwards towards the door. 'Did you see that?' she demanded. Bob had heard the clatter of the pen landing but hadn't actually seen it and I had caught no more than a fleeting glimpse of something red darting by us. Leaning forwards, I picked up the pen. Considering that it hadn't been used since the last class some hours before, the object should have been cold. However, this pen was warm.

Taking into account where it had landed, I estimated its possible course of trajectory to originate from the far right-hand corner of the classroom. Checking the entire room for any unusual temperature changes or electrical charges, Bob then informed us of an incident reported by a young boy inmate from Woburn's borstal years who had sworn that his bedding was pulled clear of his bed one night by a tall, ghostly shadow. According to Bob, the bed once stood in the very space we now occupied in the classroom.

Tea and ghosts

A rational open mind is essential for any investigator of the paranormal, for with each witness account taken one has to allow the facts to take precedence over the supernatural. However, once in a while a witness comes along whose strong-willed, logical mind is in constant denial following a brush with the paranormal.

Ask any tough, disciplined drill sergeant if he believes in ghosts and his response would probably be a harsh order to perform 100 push-ups followed by a day in the mess toilets with a toothbrush. Luckily this particular drill officer had already encountered the ghost of Woburn first hand on his very first day at the prison officer training college.

Taking his leave on an early morning tea break, the sergeant made himself comfortable in one of the small tearooms and proceeded to read his newspaper, having first shut the door. The door itself was held firmly closed by a heavy duty spring, so upon hearing the sound of the door opening, he glanced up to see who it was. An eerie silence filled the room. Nobody was there and to his astonishment, the spring-back door, which should have immediately slammed itself shut with no one there to restrain it, remained wide open. Confused, he made his way toward the open doorway, calling out to ask who was there. As he reached the door his blood froze, for there in front of him barring his exit a freezing cold mist emerged. Regaining his composure, the officer stepped through the mist emerging in the corridor outside shivering, chilled to the bone. The violent slam of the door behind him finally broke his nerve and hastily he made his way back to his colleagues, expecting ridicule. To his surprise, however, the other officers reacted calmly to his story informing him that he had probably just met 'the butler'.

The well

With all haunted houses, the stories generally far outweigh any factual evidence, but with Marion's arrival the next morning, the house and the alleged ghosts within appeared to be of no interest to her. Ignoring the front door she made her way towards what used to be the servants quarters coming to a halt at the far left-hand corner of the mansion house.

'I have a young woman here with me,' she began, 'about 20 to 25 years of age. She was calling to me as soon as I arrived.' It had to be the servant girl. Of course, I knew the story, but Marion didn't even know where she was, having been driven in secrecy to the location by our production manager so there was no possible way that she could have obtained any prior information. 'She's telling me she's in the well … underwater in the well and she says that she was murdered.'

With no sign of a well anywhere on the site, I had to admit that this wasn't looking good, but to be sure I approached the one person who would certainly know, Bob Pue. He informed me that there had indeed been a well, bricked up without trace over 150 years ago. The big question was: could Marion find it?

Without saying a word, Bob and I accompanied Marion around the entire building where along the way she picked up the presence of a man, who she thought must have been important in status within the household simply due to his commanding personality, but at no point did she confirm that this was Barkley, the butler. However, in her opinion the man was definitely not a member of the family. Very tall, well groomed and very suspicious of her, the mysterious ghost never left her side throughout her entire walkabout.

I never knew the whereabouts of the well; only Bob had this knowledge, so how Marion walked straight to its hidden location in the main ground floor front room that once served as a dining room was creepy to say the least. Standing there she pointed downwards, stating, 'Here, it's here and there's a tunnel leading from the well straight out under the house to the beach.'

Bob confirmed all that Marion had found. Checking the historical records of the house, we soon found the original plans of the property revealing the location of the well and the tunnel exactly where she had sensed them to be. A butler named Robert Barkley also turned up in the Millisle census records of 1901. A married Catholic man, any affair resulting in a pregnancy would have greatly opposed his religion and destroyed his family name; so had we had found a motive for the alleged murder of the maid?

Unfortunately, no record could be found connecting this particular Barkley to Woburn House, and furthermore, no mention of a murder or suicide had been filed anywhere in the record books. So we were left with two possibilities: either the Butler and the maid was just a local tale, or this shameful episode from Woburn's past had been covered up by the household to avoid embarrassment. It was time for answers and since none was forthcoming from the library records, our only option was to attempt to root out the elusive butler from his spiritual hideaway.

The team began with a frequency sweep in the tower room utilising a method whereby one single tone was emitted ranging from infrasound that operates at around 20HZ right up to ultrasound 20,000HZ, both of which are beyond the normal human hearing range. The aim of the experiment was to try and introduce a frequency that the ghosts could hear and possibly communicate on. In simplistic terms, we were sending out an electronic SOS.

Investigating Woburn House

Although no voices came forward, Mark, our sound technician, did record a distinct, low, base tone at 3,000HZ, not once, but three times, indicating a possible response. Interesting, but inconclusive. The next step was to put my ghost nest idea into operation.

The ghost nest

The excitement was intense, because the night ahead promised to be a step back to the good old-fashioned ghost hunting methods used by our predecessors. For this investigation, the entire team from the Northern Ireland Paranormal Society would be brought in mainly to assist in monitoring the CCTV camera screens. My plan

The ghost nest vigil

for the night was to set up a cluster of controlled object tests in an area where most activity had been reported. From witness accounts taken earlier that day, the ghost appeared to have a repetitive pathway, walking down the first-floor corridor, along the passage and up the staircase branching off to Bob's office in the tower. Ordering CCTV cameras to be placed in the tower room, the far corridor and the lower landing ensured that if anything was to walk this route or make a sound during the night, it would certainly be captured and relayed back to our main base station located out of the way in a back storeroom on the top floor.

When looking for ghosts, it helps if you can understand their way of thinking, so rather than introducing them to alien, 21st-century equipment such as thermal imaging cameras, EMF devices and infrared beams alone, I informed the team that all of our equipment be carefully placed and hidden where possible. For this to work, the ghost had to feel at ease and unthreatened, so the idea was to create a scene that a person from the 19th century could relate to. Once surrounded by recognisable items, the hope was that this would induce some kind of reaction such as a movement, a temperature drop or, better still, intelligent communication.

With a table now placed on the lower landing all that remained was for the following items to be placed upon it:

- An open Bible
- A lit candle placed in a 19th-century candle holder
- A 19th-century dinner bell
- A sheet of writing paper with a fountain pen
- One large glass of brandy.

Close-range microphones were then attached to the banisters with an EMF meter in the centre of the table beside the Bible. Sound checks were then made to ensure any noise made up in the control room by a member of the team, including echoes, would not be picked up on the short-range microphones downstairs in the ghost nest. By 9pm all was set, and with every last team member tightly squeezed into the control room the vigil could begin. Apart from us, Woburn House was now empty.

Paranormal investigations are notorious for being boring once the levels of expectation drift away and the hours pass by with nothing happening, but at least we had a three-man BBC film crew to record us yawning into the small hours. With the exception of the candle flickering in the dark, the ghost nest monitors remained free of activity, so I was pulled to one side by the director and asked to give an account of what I expected to happen during the night ahead.

With my head now in presenter mode, my concentration was abruptly distracted by a faint noise from the lower levels of the house. Booming up from the corridors below, voices echoed up and down the vacant mansion causing us all to stop whatever we were doing and check that nobody had moved out of the control room and headed downstairs. Mark responded by radio informing me that everybody was present and that the sound appeared to be a television set coming from somewhere within the house. Moving out on to the darkened landing I peered over the edge to get a better listen, instantly confirming for myself that it was the sound of a TV.

But who or what had switched it on?

Everybody was ushered back into the control room and as we all huddled around, Mark turned up the volume on the speakers. Faint footsteps, knockings and whispers emanating from the floors below, as if challenging us to descend the stairs to investigate, now became more audibly apparent. Motioning to Tony, the sceptic of the team, to follow me, I grabbed a torch and together we descended the stairway, making our way carefully past the ghost nest and into the corridors beyond.

All was still as we began to check every room in search of the elusive television. The first place I entered was the mess room where I knew a big widescreen set stood, but the screen was cold. The set had been switched off for some time. Leaving Tony to check the kitchens, I made my way down more stairs, whilst by radio reminding Mark in the control room to keep an eye on the ghost nest. In the back of my mind, was the thought that this whole caper could be a crafty diversion.

Making my way by torchlight along Woburn's empty passageways, a noise began to filter through the din some distance away in front of me. It sounded like a steady wooden knocking and the closer I drew myself to it the more intense the atmosphere in this old building became. The source of the sound appeared to be in the main room at the front of the house, the room that had been built over the well. Opening the big oak door, I made my way in. The darkened room consciously increased my edgy mood for within its gloom, the banging noises seemed ever so slightly threatening. Step by step, I moved forward towards the large bay windows and located an unfastened wooden shutter rapping against the window pane. The moment I reached out to silence it, the movement stopped.

Breathing a sigh of relief I checked for any evidence of an open window that could account for a draught of air and sure enough I found one. However, the night was still with hardly any breeze. Poking the heavy shutter with my fingers I watched it knock the pane once before coming to a standstill. With an eyebrow raised, I decided to leave this little mystery for another time and head back into the building to search for the elusive television.

Before I reached the door, a voice whispered from behind me, 'Help me.' Swinging around, the light from my torch arched up and down the room searching each corner for a human figure that simply wasn't there. Walking back to the centre of the room I came to a stop directly over the space where the well had once stood and asked the voice to repeat what it had just said.

Tony returned from his sweep of the building with nothing to report and since no further response had been forthcoming from the well room, I decided to keep the incident to myself. The sound of the television had now been joined by muffled male Irish voices and having once located the source, the answer to all of this became very clear. The sounds were not coming from inside the building at all, but we were hearing them via the intercom system speakers dotted all round the mansion house.

Within the space of five minutes we were all having a good laugh with the security guards who had accidentally placed a paperback book on to the 'on' switch for the intercom located inside their cabin just a short distance away from the house by the main gate. Little known to them, their private conversation, together with a BBC1 soap courtesy of their portable television set, had been broadcasting around the 17th-century manor for over 20 minutes. A fun-filled wild goose chase, yes, but at least a logical explanation had been found.

Relaxed yet a little disappointed, I advised Mark back at control of the false alarm, but his response set my enthusiasm alight once again and we ran back towards the house, my mind churned over his last comments. The instruments in the ghost nest were flashing, meaning the EMF meter and the digital thermometer were registering electromagnetic and temperature fluctuations. Even more exciting, the CCTV camera in the tower room had filmed what appeared to be a bright ghostly hand shooting across the office. Pacing the stairs like a gazelle, Tony and I reached the control room in seconds and reviewed the footage recorded. What struck me as odd was that all of this activity had started the moment we had left the house leaving just Mark, Marion and Julia Irvine to hold the fort. Coincidence again?

The screen shot of the live picture feedback from the ghost nest was showing fleeting shadows across the Bible, but this was difficult to accept as paranormal due to the flickering candlelight, but the shot of a shooting hand-like image recorded up in the tower room was immensely impressive.

Explanations were bandied about the team. Firstly, could it be a moth or another insect? This was unlikely for the object was rectangular in shape and too large and fast for any conventional insect, and besides, the room had been checked for insects before the experiment commenced. Could it perhaps be a flake of paint dropping from the ceiling? Again, a possibility. However, later checks revealed no sign of flaking paint anywhere in the room. Rather than labelling the anomaly as paranormal, the team took the vote to file it as unexplainable.

Believing something to be there, Marion began openly to ask any entities present to acknowledge their existence. Seated by the storeroom door, her questions filtered down the staircase to the ghost nest, where almost immediately the microphones began to pick up a moderate response.

No recognisable words could be heard, but the audio wave was clearly showing a static, repeatable pattern every time a question was asked. Initially I assumed this had to be an echo of Marion's voice, until we asked the unknown visitor to knock twice. Two static responses came back, so to be sure we repeated the experiment three times. On all three occasions, two static knocks were delivered

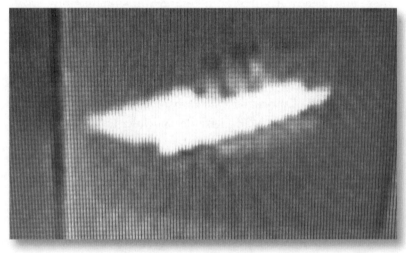

A screenshot of the strange light anomaly captured in the tower room

proving that this was not a result of an echo being picked up by our microphones downstairs, but to lay this to rest finally, I rapped a rhythm of knocks on the table. Should all of this be the result of an echo then logically, the sound would be picked up and relayed back to the wave player. It was not.

According to Marion, Woburn had three ghosts, one female and two males, all of whom were aware of each other. The legend, though, remained and since none of us would ever know if the knocks from the ghost nest originated from the butler, our final attempt to close the case rested with the medium, so before we left Woburn I asked Marion to contact the girl one last time.

It was a warm sunny morning for Bob Pue who at last was hoping to discover the truth behind the infamous story of the servant girl and Barkley. A medium can do many things, but forcing a sprit to come forward against its will is not one of them. Happily, though, on this occasion, the servant girl needed no encouragement. Bringing the legend to light, Marion proceeded to tell the story as told by the ghost of the maid.

The girl's name was Ann. She was a servant for the household, but her early pregnancy had cast a shadow over her once happy life. Neither her parents nor her employers had any knowledge of her condition and sadly her last desperate chance of salvation had been brutally extinguished by her lover, the baby's father, who wanted nothing to do with her. Following an emotional last plea, her lover's patience ran out and in a fit of rage he murdered her, submitting her lifeless body to the depths of Woburn's well.

Rumours that Ann had run away in shame provided an alibi for the murderer, whose crime went unpunished, but the ghost remained and finally it was revealed that the butler was innocent. Barkley had nothing to do with her death and although Marion pressed for the murderer's true identity, Ann stayed silent, even in death protecting the man she so obviously loved all those years ago.

The Matron and the Round Room

Limavady has a workhouse
Nobody wants to go in
Don't go into the workhouse
You'll never get out again.

The investigation of Limavady Workhouse, October 2008

Meaning 'Leap of the dog' in Irish, Limavady is located in the north-west of Ireland not far from Londonderry and is the birthplace of the most famous Irish song, 'Danny Boy'. Its name originates from the legend of a dog owned by a chief of the O'Cahans who jumped a gorge on the river Roe, alerting the clan of an impending attack.

Limavady Workhouse operated from 1842 to 1932 and was no holiday camp. If you were destitute back in those days there were no social security payouts, no council housing, so as a last resort, simply for the sake of survival, the poor would find themselves walking down the long, foreboding road towards the workhouse, where a life of misery and harsh punishment awaited.

Upon arrival, husbands and wives were separated and the children taken away. Stripped of their clothes, hosed down and provided with workhouse attire, days of hardship with barely enough food to survive was the best that anyone could hope for. Some children as young as two were put to work in the fields, while

Limavady Workhouse

others, in the event of their parents' death, were shipped to Australia. The reason why this regime was so harsh was to dissuade those looking for a free, easy life in the care of the government. If you had enough to survive on your own, then the workhouse was not for you.

The potato famine

Beginning in 1845 and lasting for six long years, the potato famine claimed over a million Irish lives. With a further million people fortunate enough to have the funds to flee the country, Ireland was facing the worst disaster in its history. The famine began in September 1845 when disease began to appear on the leaves of potato plants causing then to turn black, curl and then rot. It was thought that this was the result of a fog that had drifted across the fields of Ireland. However, the real cause turned out to be an airborne fungus called *phytophthora infestans* that had spawned in the holds of ships sailing from North America to England.

As thousands began to starve, families found themselves turned out of their homes by mounting debt leaving them homeless and penniless, which resulted in many simply dying in the streets. In these desperate times, workhouses were over run and for those who did manage to make it there alive on foot, the workhouse was certainly not their salvation, as the average life expectancy for the worst cases was one week.

The ghosts

In April 1930, the remaining inmates were transferred to Coleraine Workhouse and the building was converted into the Limavady District Hospital in 1933. Since then, the building has been home to a number of ghost stories, many of which are believed even by the hardy security guards. They claim that they regularly hear the sound of crying babies coming from the old, disused maternity ward on the first floor, and one security guard, Evan Hand, is convinced that he encountered the ghost of a matron walking up the stairs.

Other sightings dating back to the 1960s and 1970s have been of a nurse dressed in an old-fashioned cape with a red hood sitting on the bridge at the front of the hospital. The central ghost story is one of a pregnant nurse who, having delivered the baby herself, smothered the child in order to keep her pregnancy a secret. Guilt and panic soon took hold and shortly afterwards she is said to have hanged herself.

The eerie setting of the dormitory

General Manager Damien Corr is in agreement with many of the staff at Limavady that the focal ghost who walks and protects the building is the founder of the hospital, Dr Katherine Robertson, whose portrait hangs in the reception hall. She is said to visit dying patients and has been seen holding the hands of the terminally ill moments before they pass away.

The investigation

With such a multitude of different stories and areas to investigate, I decided to bring in the Northern Ireland Paranormal Society earlier than usual and as they set up their sophisticated selection of recording and detection equipment, Marion arrived to begin her psychic evaluation of the location.

Her first port of call was a recently uncovered dormitory dating back to the days of the workhouse that had been bricked up for over 100 years. I had spent some time in there earlier that day listening to Damien relay the history of those dreadful years, but despite being historically beautiful and untouched, the room contained no evidence of a haunting. However, Marion could feel the anguish, the pain and the suffering that had infested the room all those years ago. She described the dormitory as holding a residual memory, an echo from the past rather than a conscious haunting.

In the days of the workhouse, the area had been witness to people dropping dead where they stood, packed in like sardines on straw bedding, diseased, mistreated and, one would imagine, praying for death. With sunlight now bathing the room, this former hellhole now resembled an area of peace, producing an aura of tranquillity similar to that of a church.

The matron

Our next port of call was the area where Evan Hand had witnessed a ghostly shadow of a matron walk past his office before making its way up the staircase. Once again, Marion had no knowledge of the stories associated with the building and in such a vast place the chances of her coming across a particular area where ghosts had been reported was beyond the realms of coincidence.

We had walked up many corridors and through countless doors until finally we reached our destination. Far from being distinct, the corridor and stairway was a facsimile of every other stairway we had passed and so bore no suggestion of its importance to the medium. Leading the way up the staircase, however, Marion soon discovered the secret I had been holding back from her. A little hesitantly, she stopped halfway up searching for an answer to the question her mediumistic side had obviously challenged her with.

Eyes closed, she surveyed the empty landing with her sixth sense, until finally she told me that a nurse was with her. She continued to say that the spirit appeared to hold some authority and suggested that perhaps she was a matron. I felt like jumping up and down with delight for she had found the exact area the ghost was supposed to walk and clarified its identity without having any prior information of the layout of the hospital or indeed the story told to us by the security guard. She continued, describing her uniform and her uncanny resemblance to Barbra Streisand, and finished by connecting the spirit to the 1940s or early 1950s.

The scratches

So far every investigation, every haunted house and every entity we appeared to have encountered had been benign. Some had displayed emotions such as anger, fear or confusion, but on the whole no physical act of assault had been reported; so it was with much surprise when one of the team, Roddy Breslin, walked into the control room stating that he felt he had been scratched.

The proof was there, two fresh scratches just below his shoulder blades and plainly out of reach of his own fingers, which immediately ruled out the possibility of self-harm. Bedsides, Roddy was a trusted and experienced team member, and after some debate we were all satisfied that he was telling the truth.

For anybody to be harmed by an entity is generally deemed to be impossible, since a ghost has no physical body to command such an act. However, taking into account the thousands of poltergeist reports that are filed each year from around the world, one has to accept that if entities can move solid objects then logically they must also have the ability to touch and perhaps wound a living person. Limavady certainly held a dark, bleak past, but nobody had sensed anything threatening in the atmosphere that could account for this kind of behaviour. However, from this point on we all began to tread a little more cautiously.

Investigating Limavady

To see a ghost, you either have to be in the right place at the right time or be mediumistically aware. It is said that ghosts are all around us, invisible to the naked eye, stuck in a dimension, a void that exists between the here and now. They are not always aware of our presence, just as we are not always aware of them but if they are

Andy and Marion outside Limavady workhouse

indeed there, perhaps light is the reason they remain invisible. Darren Ansel had a theory based upon the workings of the human eye.

Principally he explained to me that colour blindness can be an asset in the military especially to certain soldiers in the field of camouflaged combat and if we flood a room with ultraviolet light we may expand beyond our visual limitations and in effect see an apparition. Fanciful stuff and although Marion was not impressed with the theory, believing as she does that any light, pink, red or green, makes no difference, we were here to test out all of these theories, no matter how incomprehensible they were.

The experiment ran for 40 minutes with Marion and Darren, bathed in ultraviolet light, positioned at the foot of the staircase where the matron reputedly roams. From the control centre in the dining room, myself and sound technician Mark Cowden observed and recorded every image and sound picked up by our locked-off detection equipment, strategically placed directly behind where Marion had sensed the ghost earlier that afternoon.

To try and cause some kind of reaction, Marion called out for help stating that a nurse was urgently needed for an emergency. Her voice echoed up and down the long-disused corridors creating a whirlpool of sound on the frequency monitors. The screen displaying the experiment, however, remained clear of any ghostly images forming within the ultraviolet mix, and as time ticked by it began to dawn on us that nothing was going to happen.

Marion insisted that the energy of the matron was there on the landing watching us and although we respectfully believed she sensed something, none us was aware of any apparition. I suggested by radio that she ask the spirit to make a noise. Stepping forward the medium called out, 'Matron, nurse, can you tap on the window?' Almost instantly, a resounding tap from the window above her was clearly heard and recorded.

We had all heard it, but the big question on all of our lips was: could it have been caused by a bird or large moth hitting the pane outside, or was this really a paranormal response to Marion's question? Either way, that the tap should occur at exactly the time the request was made was an extreme coincidence. Some of us believed, others were unsure, but the next chapter in this case would embrace us all in a way nobody could ever have foreseen.

Caught on camera

It started with lights, not exactly orb-like in appearance but still moving at great speed emerging from the walls and light fittings up on the first floor close to the old maternity ward. My first impression was that it had to be a moth caught in the light of the night vision camera. However, moths don't disappear through solid walls. Going by the footage we recorded, we estimated the anomaly's speed to be around 40–50kmp/25–30mph, far too quick for any conventional insect.

The landing was dark and spooky but nonetheless exciting. Making my way up by torchlight, I kept in constant walkie-talkie contact so I could be alerted if anything resembling what we had seen were to reappear. Waving a dinner tray under all of the light fittings, picture frames and other suspected areas that any insect would hide was an amusing sight for the team downstairs, but the current of air produced would certainly have been sufficient to alert the razor-sharp senses of any moth, fly or bug and cause it to take off in search of a more secure place. Nothing happened; no speeding light anomalies appeared, just gentle floaters, dust particles stirred up by my dinner tray antics, which are often mistaken for paranormal phenomena.

The unexplainable has an annoying habit of entertaining you when you least expect it. The tea was brewed, the biscuits were out, it was time to relax and chat about football, holidays and other non-essential topics of debate. The control room was a hubbub of chitchat, so it was with some alarm that we all suddenly heard a high-pitched scream. Everybody stopped in mid-sentence, frozen stiff as if caught in the frame of a photograph, frowning with puzzlement, waiting for the sound to return. Seconds later it did just that and every person present who was a parent instantly recognised the noise. Somewhere from the rooms above, a baby was crying.

Pandemonium set in as investigators rushed for the on switch of their recording devices whilst the remainder of the team began tearing up the stairs in a frantic search of the upper rooms. No explanation was ever found, we were alone in the building and wonder soon turned to extreme disappointment as news came that no one had reacted fast enough to enable the sensory recording equipment. We had missed it, one of the biggest pieces of evidence to date had passed us by. I don't think any of us slept well that night.

The restless apparition

The cameras had been left running at the location throughout the night and next morning still rather disgruntled, Darren, Mark, Tony and I began the long vigil hunched over the digital video playback, sipping coffee hoping something would turn up. Four areas had been covered: the rooms above where the baby had been heard; the tower where a nurse had supposedly hanged herself; the corridor; and the landing vantage point that looked down the matron's stairway.

The time code read 3am when something caught Tony's eye. Rewinding it, we could hardly believe our eyes for there, through the window outside of the building opposite the exact spot where sightings of the matron had been reported, was what appeared to be a walking apparition.

The first port of call was the security guard's office to enquire if any cars had driven in during the night. The possibility of the apparition being a reflection of headlights was immediately ruled out since the gates to the complex are securely locked from midnight to 7am. Furthermore, the area where the 'ghost' disappeared through the wall turned out to be the site of an old doorway, bricked up some 20 years ago. Had Limavady Workhouse finally given up one of its paranormal secrets?

Conclusion

Looking back now, I have to say that the footage is still unexplainable when you take into account the facts surrounding the events that night. With the exception of a security guard sitting in his office totally unaware of what had flashed by our cameras, coupled with the fact that no cars could enter the through the gates, I was left with a wide selection of evidence to mull over. A tap on the window, a baby crying on an empty landing, the light anomalies and the inexplicable sight of a ghostly apparition walking through an old bricked-up doorway lead me to conclude that Limavady Workhouse was indeed haunted.

A break in filming at Limavady

The round room

Situated two miles off the main Belfast to Londonderry road, Bellaghy Bawn, meaning cattle fort, was constructed around 1614 by John Rowley. Although it is suspected that there were Celtic settlements in the area beforehand, Bellaghy was one of the first planned towns in Ireland. The village itself dates back to the 17th century, when it was one of many towns built under the authority of the Vintners Company of London as part of the plantation of Derry.

During the 1641 rebellion, the original bawn was virtually destroyed and the greater part of Bellaghy burnt to the ground. During the siege, Henry Conway brought all his local paying settlers of the Bellaghy village inside the bawn walls to protect them from the Irish who were on the rampage. A local division of Irish troops led by Peter O'Hagan soon arrived at the gates to take the bawn by force. Conway went outside to negotiate with the troops and instead made a personal deal with O'Hagan, ensuring a safe escape for himself and his family. Conway was never seen again. He left the local residents to their own devices against the Irish onslaught.

The round room at Bellaghy Bawn

The bawn was rebuilt in 1643 and lasted until 1791 when a totally new structure was built in its place. Only one of the original flanker towers still remains today and despite reports of hazy apparitions, ghostly footsteps and other such phenomena being reported around the building, my instincts led me straight to the oldest part of the structure, the flanker tower that is home to the round room.

My visit to Bellaghy had been as restful as a three-day break from the woes of rush hours and school runs. The sun was shining, the air was warm and the serenity of the countryside around glowed amidst the backdrop of country life. So far no paranormal activity had occurred and although Marion had clearly sensed the fire that destroyed the bawn in the 17th century, even she had failed to connect with any inhabiting ghosts from within.

The whole atmosphere around the Bawn seemed to be one of a stubborn refusal to provide us with any of the information we were there to seek.

Is there anybody there?

Tentatively I stepped into the round room, a beautifully carpeted haven of peaceful splendour that could easily be mistaken for a small chapel. The room was illuminated by the bright Sunday morning sunshine that beamed through the six large windows spaced equally around the circular structure. Striding slowly forward to the centre and soaking up the atmosphere, I became aware of movement behind me. Turning around, I caught a glimpse or impression of a blue evening gown, but the whole incident was so brief I assumed it had to be a trick of the light.

Alone and with time on my hands, I produced my digital recorder, sat cross-legged in the centre of the floor and commenced an EVP experiment. For 10 minutes I asked a variety of standard questions until, like a thought emerging from my mind, I sensed a presence. There was a child, a small boy perhaps nine or ten years old but this was different, for I had never come across an image so clear that refused to talk. In my mind's eye, he just stood close to the centre of this magnificent room, mute, giving nothing away about his identity or standing in the house.

I tried dowsing to glean information but gained little success, so I offered a number of names: John, Henry, Patrick; but it wasn't until I asked the question, 'Is your name Peter?' that the dowsing rods crossed indicating the answer yes. That was it, no more information was coming forward. In fact, the presence I originally felt had long since gone, so I asked one more question: 'Is the boy still here?' The rods remained still.

Andy in the round room

All of this had been recorded, but listening to the white noise on the playback moments later, the word 'No' hissed back at me in response to both enquiries. Did this mean that the boy's name wasn't Peter and that he wasn't here any more and, if so, who had spoken for him? On the one hand I had a very interesting EVP, whilst on the other hand I had a riddle, one that would unfortunately never be resolved.

The voices in the round room were a mystery and even the paranormal team recorded a peculiar message when asking if there was a woman called Susan present. One would expect the answer 'yes' to such a question, but to receive the response 'You're a hooker' followed by a series of knocks made no sense whatsoever. But when searching for evidence of a haunting, any EVPs once cleared of natural interference are considered gold dust, no matter what the voice appears to be saying.

Of all the areas supposedly haunted at Bellaghy Bawn, the round room was the focal point, a cocoon for the remaining energies within to continue to exist until the day the building is no more. On my final day, I returned to the room with my digital recorder simply to say farewell and to offer my thanks. Upon reviewing the recording later that day, my voice can be heard saying the words, 'Thank you.' Seconds later, a young girl's whisper breaks the silence. As if in acknowledgement she replies, 'Capitaine', meaning captain in French.

Since I had been leading the investigations in Ireland for the past three months, perhaps in her eyes I was the team's captain? Additionally, history reads that in the year 1700, French Huguenots refugees fled to Northern Ireland to settle and were responsible for the founding of the great Irish linen industry, which began just a short distance from Bellaghy.

Yet another coincidence?

Galgorm Castle

Up until now, EVPs had always materialised on audio as distorted words hidden deep within static or white noise, but during our final case in Northern Ireland an EVP was recorded that was uniquely different from any piece of paranormal evidence I had ever heard before. This time it had spoken to us not through a microphone or via a frequency sweep, but directly into our ears, leaving me stunned with a cascade of speculative thoughts.

After months of experimentation, had we at last formed an understanding, an empathy with whatever lay hidden on the other side of life?

The history of Galgorm

Built by Sir Faithful Fortescue in 1618, Galgorm Castle in County Antrim is perhaps the finest example of Jacobean architecture in Ireland. The site covers over 200 acres incorporating remnants of an ancient Irish fort belonging to the McQuillan clan, together with the castle's chapel, burnt down in 1798 by the United Irishmen.

The Young family, who bought the estate in 1843, were known as pioneers of their time, as they ensured prosperity of the estate by introducing new farming methods, such as constructing flax dams and a water wheel. This made Galgorm one of the foremost agricultural estates in Northern Ireland, employing over 30 staff to maintain the house, the stables and the farm.

In the 1900s, with the introduction of the industrial revolution, new mechanised farming methods began to affect the estate's wealth and as a result Galgorm went into decline.

Galgorm Castle

Dr Coalville, the clerical wizard

Originally of Norman descent, the Coalvilles arrived in England during the invasion of William the Conqueror with one branch of the family settling in Scotland in the 12th century. Alexander Colville was ordained in 1622 and came to Ireland in 1650 to become the founder of the Irish branch of the Coalville family.

Appointed to the Rectory of Skerry in 1654, he became a Doctor of Divinity and remained in mid-Antrim until his death in 1679. At first, Alexander drew a modest income but gradually he amassed a vast fortune, creating a divide between himself and the

The portrait of Dr Coalville

local Presbyterians, whose ministers he railled against as intruders of the ministry and the province. Using his wealth to obtain 21 town lands caused a great deal of local jealousy and enticed many of his neighbours to spread a rumour that he had sold himself to the devil in exchange for gold and that he could raise Satan at will.

With witchcraft and the dark arts very much a strong belief, Alexander soon found himself shunned and over time the story about his supposed amoral exploits evolved into legend.

The legend of the doctor and the devil

The story goes that late one evening the doctor was fishing on the banks of the river Maine not far from his own house when he noticed somebody close by. Turning around, he saw a dark stranger who enquired if he had any luck of late, to which the doctor replied with a mournful no. The stranger was the devil in human form and granted the doctor a boot full of gold in return for the deliverance of his soul in 21 years. An agreement was made and the deal was arranged to take place at Coalville's house, where the doctor succeeded in cheating the devil by cutting the sole from his boot and placing it over a hole in the floor above the basement. The devil kept his word, continuing to fill the boot until Coalville's cellar was stacked high with a fortune of gold. Realising he had been tricked, the devil took his leave, promising to return in 21 years to collect on the bargain.

But when the stranger arrived once again in the Coalville's drawing room, the doctor managed to trick him once again. 'Your time is up, Alexander Coalville. Now come with me quietly,' said the devil. The doctor was reading the Bible by candlelight and begged the devil to give him until the last piece of the candle burnt out. The devil reluctantly agreed, unaware of the scheming Doctor's next move. Knowing that the devil is forbidden to place his hand on the holy book, Coalville blew out the candle, placing the remaining stub within the pages of the Bible before closing the book shut.

With the last piece of the candle now forever prevented from burning, the devil disappeared empty handed never to return.

A curse in the guise of Coalville's portrait supposedly hangs in the entrance hallway of Galgorm and it is said that if the painting were ever to be removed, tragedy would once again befall the estate.

The castle guard

The bleak outline of Galgorm Castle on a crisp November morning set amidst the silhouette of lifeless-looking autumn trees sent an excited shiver down my spine as my car passed slowly through the castle's huge gothic entrance gates. I parked at the end of the long drive, pausing for a moment to take in the ambience of the scene facing me. The structure of the building was intact, with all sign of refurbishment hidden from sight by intertwining ivy that crept up the face of the castle walls like a spider's web. Daunting as it was, the castle and its grounds still retained the majesty of its bygone days with only Galgorm's chapel fallen by the wayside, leaving behind a vague reminder of its once profound presence.

The belief of divine protection within the boundaries of consecrated ground is mainly connected to church sites, so to discover a barrier of energy surrounding a castle could mean one of two things: either it had been put there as a result of some ancient pagan ritual to keep evil spirits at bay, or at some point in Galgorm's past the site had been blessed by the early priesthood. Needless to say, my curiosity was soon aroused as just a few steps away from the castle walls a field of energy alerted my senses. Although considered unscientific, my only course of detecting this barrier was through divining rods, and so before I even contemplated entering, I spent 15 minutes outside, mapping the size and course of the energy field circulating the building.

The barrier covered not only the house but also a small percentage of the immediate grounds, essentially cocooning the property in the shape of an oval. Surprisingly, the interior of the castle radiated tranquillity, a warmth that owner Christopher Brooke said had been commented upon by almost every visitor. Obviously aware of the castle's dark legend, Christopher noted that he, too, felt the place to be protected perhaps by the infamous Doctor Coalville himself, whose portrait stared down at me from its vantage point in the entrance hallway. According to legend, whoever removed the painting would instigate a curse upon himself and the estate. But looking into the eyes of Coalville, I found this hard to believe because his face brought forth a kindness, totally alien to the dark tale associated with him. However, one had to wonder what secrets lay behind that placid stare.

The only indication I personally had of any ghosts at this point was the vague impression of an elderly woman, although for some reason the age she gave me contradicted her appearance, for in my mind's eye, I could see a young girl in her prime. Strangely enough, the shy ghost had not entered the building with me, but instead veered off to the left of the courtyard before vanishing from my senses, perhaps the result of the field of energy barring her way.

In contrast, the courtyard, part of which dates back to the early 17th century, once suffered the indignity of an attempted conversion using Victorian architecture and as a result many of the original walls were demolished. Renovations are a classic common cause of many hauntings, so a radical change such as this could easily confuse and even prevent any lingering ghosts from passing through areas they no longer recognise from their time. Continuing to tour the castle with Christopher, I soon shrugged off the notion for if there was indeed a trapped spirit stuck outside then Marion would pick this up in greater detail when she arrived.

The castle was in need of renovation, notably the third and fourth floors, but its living quarters on the lower levels perfectly matched the old saying 'An Englishman's home is his castle'. Christopher had never encountered anything remotely paranormal himself, although his young son had reported seeing a man wearing a long, black coat roaming the corridors. Previous to this, his grandmother also stated that she hade been woken one night by the spectral image of a maid who begged her to follow her out on to the landing where, unbeknown to anyone, Christopher's grandfather, having failed to extinguish his pipe properly in the dustbin before retiring to bed, had started a fire.

With this potential tragedy averted, from that day forward the grandmother regarded the ghost as Galgorm's saviour, something that appeared to be correct when shortly afterwards the maid returned again one night to warn her that the horses had escaped and were galloping through Ballymena. Without stopping to check the stables, she drove straight into town to find her horses on the loose. Christopher's grandmother was by no means prone to fanciful delusions and despite her being a woman of no nonsense she continued to believe that the phantom maid was the castle's guardian until the day she died. Personally I adore ghost stories such as this for they are far removed from the clichéd Hollywood depiction of dark evil spirits out for blood. Even the legends of Doctor Coalville's dealings with the devil have a more rational explanation if you care to study the history books.

The doctor was a royalist, despised by his local Presbyterians and back in the 17th century the quickest and most common procedure for tarnishing a wealthy royalist such as Coalville would be either to concoct shameful rumours of fornication with a married woman or spread the word that the said gentlemen was dabbling in witchcraft. In fact, the only dabbling Coalville had a tendency to entertain was his passion for alchemy. Rich in history but poor in facts, the legend of Galgorm hangs over the castle like a dark cloud, epitomised by flocks of crows that sour the night sky over the castle's heights as dusk falls.

Christopher's hospitality far exceeded my expectations and although his love for the family home was very apparent, the sad fact that Galgorm was in need of financial rescue cast a shadow over the investigation, for the beauty of this place shone brightly amidst the sorrowful demise of its once majestic splendour.

Secrets of the key

I was due to meet Marion before she arrived at the location and so decided to take the opportunity to test her once again. For my first experiment I required an item from the castle, something old and relevant that would once have been held by either Coalville himself or a trusted member of the house staff. Luckily, the original main

The film crew at Galgorm

door key over 300 years old was placed in my possession, allowing me to conduct a psychometric test with Marion in order to reveal if any part of Galgorm's past was strong enough to reach out to us beyond its barrier. Mysteriously, a little way away Marion, gripping the key with both hands, began to glean information from the object stating that the door it belonged to held a dark, silent secret and whatever that secret may be was locked inside rather than out.

Without jumping to too many conclusions, her insight mirrored my own feelings regarding the energy barrier and in hindsight perhaps I had been a little off the mark with my assumption that its presence was intended to prevent something from entering the castle. Maybe the purpose of the energy field was meant to keep something locked inside. The question was: what?

If there were any secrets to be found lurking behind Galgorm's doors, then now was the time to commence our search. Evening was approaching and as we walked slowly down the long, lonely driveway towards the castle, a mysterious dark chill began to swirl about our feet.

Almost at once, a girl was alongside Marion, shadowing her every move. She gave her name as Rosemary and as I observed this walking conversation between the medium and the ghost, the location of the barrier grew ever closer. To my disappointment, Marion strolled undramatically past the spot, waving to the spirit who apparently left her side, stating unceremoniously that the ghost of Rosemary could not go any further due to the energy field surrounding the castle.

In the space of two hours we had toured the entire site and throughout that time there was never any suggestion of a male spirit resembling Doctor Coalville inhabiting the building. However, Marion's connection brought forward an endless stream of names, all of whom were aware of a secret never to be told.

Allowing sleeping dogs to lie, my next step involved a four-day investigation with Darren Ansel's team.

Galgorm's ghosts awake

Night one passed without incident, but with the onset of night two, the unexplained returned once again to challenge our perception of reality. The evening had started well with an experiment into the world of psychic art, a procedure where a sensitive tunes into the energies around him and sketches images of the dead.

For some time I had jostled with an image of a lady that I could not get out of my mind. It seemed no matter where I stood in the grounds of Galgorm, this lady was virtually in my face. Settling myself down with a pencil and paper by the landing window above the entrance hall, I began to draw the image in my mind. So clear was her face, her picture took just minutes to sketch and upon its completion the lady's image left my mind and she was gone, leaving not a thank you or a critical remark.

The drawing did resemble Jane Young, who was married at the castle in 1901, but due to the age and angle of the photograph there was no way to conclude this likeness ultimately for the cameras.

Occasionally, encounters with ghosts can be fleeting, lasting merely seconds before the link is broken either by choice or due to a sudden energy evaporation that is vital in order to sustain their presence. She hadn't been a seductively pretty woman, but kindly in life, passing I felt in her mid-50s, if the sketch drawn was indeed an accurate depiction of her. It seemed that nothing was about to jump out of the shadows on this case, but later, as the clock struck midnight, one of Galgorm's male hosts was to make himself known in a particularly interesting way.

Are you sure?

Earlier that afternoon, two locked-off cameras had been placed on the same landing not far from Alexander Coalville's painting and for the past 10 hours had digitally recorded the routine comings and goings of the team. Just before midnight, the images of Tony, Julia and Roddy Breslin climbing the staircase were being observed on screen by Mark Cowden in the control room. Nearing the top, Tony voiced his wish to spend a little time alone up in the attic to run some tests. Turning to Tony, Julia said, 'Are you sure?' to which he replied, 'Yeah.' At that precise moment, all three investigators are struck numb by the words of an unknown, fourth male voice whispering the words, 'Are you sure?' straight into their ears.

Shocked and confused, the trio began a frantic search of the landing for that elusive fourth person, but nobody was there. Confirming to each other that they had all heard the Irish voice at the same time, the excited team immediately reviewed the footage in the hope that the ghostly whisper had been caught on audio. It

The team listen to the ghostly voice

had and we now possessed positive proof that a disembodied voice had emerged out of thin air.

The recording was played over and over again and checked by Mark to confirm that the speech pattern did not belong to any member of the team present, thus straight away ruling out any suspicions of a hoax or echo. Armed with this remarkable evidence, Tony requested to take up the challenge left by the voice and go it alone in the darkness of the attic where the ghosts of Galgorm had dared him to venture.

The attic's masterful haunting atmosphere would be any ghost hunter's dream, but although Tony felt slightly anxious he reported feeling no sense of foreboding as he sat for over an hour and a half surrounded by hooked-up microphones and CCTV cameras.

Throughout his vigil he conducted a number of EVP experiments in case the ghostly voice had something further to say. Everything remained still and silent until, picking up his radio to check in with base, a faint male whisper drifted from the depths of the mottled cobwebs masked in the gloom. 'Don't – do – that.' Once again three words, digitally recorded, conveyed a spooky message to the investigator instructing him not to use his radio.

Tony is the youngest member of the Northern Ireland Paranormal Society and a self-confessed sceptic. However, following this and other strange occurrences he had been witness to during the making of the TV series, he was now fast becoming more convinced that there was definitely something going on that was beyond his normal level of understanding.

With all of this evidence coming to light, the team turned their attention back to the first-floor landing as this appeared to be the focal point of the phenomenon. But as they were recoiling from yet another mysterious voice, team member Roddy Breslin was about to have a brush with the unknown himself.

He never felt it, never saw it, but the orb-like anomaly could clearly be seen on the DVD playback crossing the room straight towards him. At first, the doughnut-shaped orb seemed set upon a collision course with the investigator, until at the last moment it altered its trajectory, skimming over the top of his head before disappearing out of camera shot.

One can never fully rule out moths, but this orb made no sound, no fluttering of wings or buzz as it skipped across Roddy's scalp almost brushing his ear. For a castle rich in dust particles I expected orbs a plenty. However, this singular light anomaly was interesting simply due to its speed and change of direction indicating a sense of instinct. Furthermore, the fact that no fly in existence bears the physical attributes of possessing a hole in the centre of its body ruled out the possibility of an insect.

Over the course of day three we tried a variety of experiments, including a rather disappointing exercise involving a Ouija board called 'spirit of the glass'. This provided little evidence for the team since the whole process is completely unreliable and often mistaken by enthusiasts as true evidence of spiritual contact. The glass held by five individual team members had moved in response to a variety of questions, but as with dowsing, any subconscious movement could easily account for the results gained from this demonstration.

Roddy and the orb anomaly taken from the monitor screen

The light at the end of the tunnel

Much to my delight, day three promised to reveal some real answers and a possible conclusion to the identity of the talkative ghost. Robert Coalville, the sole surviving descendent of the infamous Doctor Alexander Coalville was flying in from England bringing with him a wealth of knowledge that would hopefully shed some light on the mysterious events witnessed so far.

Upon his arrival, Robert toured the estate once owned by his ancestors with a telltale pride in his step. This was the first time a Coalville had frequented the castle for over 300 years. On the afternoon of day four, having spent his first night in his ancestral

Touring Galgorm Castle

home, Robert joined Christopher Brooke and me as we began to piece together the puzzle. The legend of Alexander Coalville is well documented and so required no further exploration. However, Robert brought to our attention the true story of a 17th-century maid who once served at the castle.

It is said that a girl from Galgorm was arrested in Scotland for crimes committed under the witchcraft act of 1603. Throughout her subsequent trial she pleaded her innocence, stating that she had never been in league with the devil and that a certain Doctor Alexander Coalville had trained her in the dark arts against her will under a spell. Her identity and subsequent fate remain a mystery.

However, the alleged secret of Galgorm reported by Marion did contain an element of historical fact that appeared to support the evidence of the EVP recorded on the first floor and the attic above. Long ago, a Captain James Coalville, on the run for some misdemeanour, took refuge in the castle and although his presence was known to the staff, they were all sworn to secrecy. The captain rarely ventured out into the grounds during daylight hours, opting instead to hide himself away on the upper levels of the castle. The reason why he was hiding remains another of Galgorm's mysteries.

Taking into account the location of the voice the team heard and recorded, could it be possible that some essence of Captain James Coalville still remains hiding in the darkened upper floors of Galgorm Castle? Although fairly circumstantial, the history certainly matched the evidence in some small way. However, when dealing with ghosts any coincidental evidence must always be subject to scrutiny.

Our time at Galgorm had been well spent and had produced enough startling footage to keep the sceptics puzzled for years to come. On 9th November 2008, our final attempt to draw out the ghosts proved unsuccessful, although an experiment with Marion placed under Coalville's portrait did produce some excessive temperature drops ranging from 13.6 degrees to 11.7 in the space of 60 seconds, proving once again that something unusual was indeed present. Unfortunately, any final attempts to speak to the spirits of Galgorm were interrupted by a local taxi firm who began broadcasting on our radio frequencies, so disappointingly the investigation was eventually abandoned due to lack of time and resources. With the end nigh, my thoughts turned to the heavens above...

Final thoughts

I stood watching the sun rise over the castle bringing forth light once again to our planet on the dawn of a new day. There are so many unknowns in our universe, millions of stars and planets of which we are but one, thrust together in space holding together billions of lives perched on the edge of forever. Why are we here stranded in the middle of the cosmos with no real answers to our own existence?

When you consider the bigger picture, life is an improbability within impossibility, for the whole of creation has no meaning, no reason for being. Logically, we shouldn't exist and science holds only theories to explain our coming to be. But here we are living our lives, ignoring those areas of reality, simply accepting our place and forever taking each day for granted.

The gases that fused what scientists call the Big Bang had to have been created by something, for such a complex concoction of life-giving energy cannot simply appear without some kind of creative force shaping its properties. Some call this creator God; others regard it as a super intelligence or higher being. The problem is we can't see it, but just because something is out of our optical range of understanding doesn't necessarily mean it isn't there. So do I believe in ghosts? In our universe anything is possible.

The answer?

Some weeks after the completion of *Northern Ireland's Greatest Haunts*, I took a nice break whilst awaiting news of series two and used the time to write this book. Alone at home, I looked back at all the evidence and experiences from the past 11 years and pondered the big question once again. Throughout my time investigating the paranormal, my one true companion when things got difficult had been the strength of my Nan whose presence never let me down.

I needed to hear the answer, not for the media, the sceptics or the cameras but for me alone. Switching on my digital recorder I spoke softly to the empty room around me.

'Nan, is there life after death? If there is, please just say yes.'

Ten seconds later listening to the playback, one single word spoken by a female voice can be clearly heard.

'Yes.'

So You Want to Hunt Ghosts?

A large percentage of hauntings are simply the work of a highly vivid imagination, so before you even contemplate entering an alleged haunted building with the sole intention of looking for a ghost, you must first have at least some understanding of what it is you are actually looking for. There are many plausible explanations for things that go bump in the night.

Although a witness may be convinced that he or she has seen, heard or felt something unusual, the first job for an investigator is to separate the normal from the paranormal. Basic tests such as checking for draughts, creaky doors, faulty plumbing, noisy water boilers and even the pet cat's squeaky cat-flap can eliminate 99% of ghostly noises immediately. However, be prepared for if you are fortunate enough to come across a genuine haunting then your knowledge and experience will be tested to the limit in deciphering and dealing with the situation.

The afterlife and God

When I am asked, 'Where is the proof of existence after death,' I generally reply, 'Open your eyes and take a look around you,' for everything that nature provides is recycled. From the demise of one living organism, sprouts a new life evolving and flourishing within its surroundings.

The concept of an almighty God is a tricky one, since the image and work of this being has been written down by mortal hand. With no apparent evidence to support this concept, it is remarkable that so many have 100% faith in religion, a subject that has through history caused more wars and race hatred than any other idealistic cause. I believe there is a God or a being of massive intellectual intelligence out there, but I think it's a far cry from what humankind has envisaged. 'God', if you like, may be part of us, the human race, a single matrix of energy maintained by the positives and negatives of the natural world. But belief in a peaceful loving God produces positive energy that in my experience, psychological or not, calms and effectively protects in a manner of reducing fear in extraordinary situations.

Mediums

Since Victorian times, mediums have claimed to have the power to contact the dead. History states that many mediums were deluding themselves and others for their own financial gain, and certainly in the years of Queen Victoria's reign many were unmasked as frauds. But now, in the 21st century, with religion offering nothing new in the way of comfort or proof, mediums are once more back in the limelight, heralding more popular belief in the afterlife than traditional Sunday church gatherings. It is an extremely difficult subject to comment upon.

If I were a total sceptic who had no knowledge or experience of mediums, then my answer would probably be, 'It's all rubbish,' and this piece would take me five minutes to write. My belief, however, is divided, for I have witnessed astounding examples of clairvoyance by mediums such as Jackie Adair and Marion Goodfellow and seen awful displays of sheer nonsense from others. The proof, if you like, is in what you want to believe. Bare facts that have been gathered by apparent channelling that match historical records later researched are interesting but inconclusive, due to the internet paving the way for easily obtained knowledge.

However, providing a total stranger with a complete rundown of his or her life incorporating jobs, problems, relationships and definitive naming of deceased relatives and their occupations and lifestyle when they were alive is altogether more baffling. Everybody has the ability, they say, everyone can do it. Well, I have on many occasions walked into a place and picked up a name or a date only to find that the information matches entirely with historical records.

I think of mediums as searchlights shining, attracting lost souls towards the light like moths to a flame, utilising their ability to raise their resonance to match each individual spirit and make contact.

The real eye-opener for me was when three family names popped into my head during an investigation at Belgrave Hall. Throughout the night I couldn't shake away the information resting at the forefront of my mind until finally, I spoke up. Led down the road to a cemetery by a member of the Association for the Scientific Study of Anomalous Phenomena (ASSAP), I was shown three graves with the names of the three I had given engraved upon the tombstones for all to see. The really weird thing is I know I wasn't cheating; I had no knowledge of the place.

Following this, for research purposes alone, I trained as a medium for two years, but after a while I found that my abilities were beginning to interfere with my intellectual reasoning on certain cases and I decided not to continue down the mediumistic path. I had, though, discovered a new-found talent in myself that I never knew was there.

I agree with mediums when they say that all life is energy and it's that part of us that ultimately survives. That particular theory is as close as we can assume to be correct if we run with the notion that we survive bodily death. Mediums shine, they attract and they have the ability to raise their resonance in order to match each individual spirit and so make contact possible. Theory or otherwise, I can neither explain nor disprove the abilities of all mediums, I let common sense see to that.

Bearing this in mind, never invite a medium to your investigation unless you either trust them or they have been recommended by somebody recognised within his or her field. There are far too many people out there attending investigations of haunted places claiming to be psychic, mediumistic or clairvoyant who are really nothing of the sort. As a result, they usually end up leading investigation teams around in circles chasing things that simply aren't there.

Before you give yourself the title of clairvoyant medium, you should have at least three to five years' training and development behind you, and be sure to remind yourself that as in all walks of life, just as there are bad mechanics and there are good mechanics, there are good and bad mediums and clairvoyants.

Psychic artists

There's an old saying that goes, 'Don't knock it 'til you've tried it.' Psychic art and automatic writing always raised an eyebrow or two for me, because I never really believed the validity of the process. After all, if automatic writing is real then how come there are no definitive cases of people writing in a language they have no knowledge of, such as a Mr Smith from Croydon writing a half-page message from a deceased Japanese man?

Psychic art, however, is a little more intriguing. Most investigators have at some point or another had a mental image of a person pop into their head during an investigation, so when it happened to me I decided to follow my instincts and sketch the image. I first tried this procedure at Chambercombe Manor back in 2002 and continue to experiment with it whenever I get a quiet moment during an investigation.

Dowsing

Another alternative to using mediums is studying the art of dowsing. Some people believe that instruments such as dowsing rods and crystal pendulums are a psychic enhancer, a tool that detects, channels and amplifies natural earth energies. In the past, dowsers were employed to find underground streams or potential coal mines, but many dowsers today believe that they can not only detect ghosts, but also, when you ask the right questions, speak to them too.

Following in the footsteps of my great uncle, I have been practically experimenting with dowsing for over eight years. He never had the modern metal version you see dowsers own today, he used the old-fashioned Y-shaped wooden sticks and his accuracy was, so I am told, quite remarkable.

Many scoff at dowsing procedures claiming repeatedly that it is not scientific in its approach and that the dowser is subconsciously moving the rods or crystal themselves. But even if this is true, then isn't that exactly how mediums work, by tuning in subconsciously to a ghost's thoughts? As we travel through space, imagine that with each step we take in life we all leave behind us an echo like an energy slipstream that can perhaps be detected for many years after or indeed for all eternity.

Whatever your views may be, results gained using this method are to say the least, interesting but still inconclusive – at least, so far. The process is simple enough, but like any other new skill, requires practice. Hold the rods out in front of you about shoulder-width apart and ask for protection and permission. The rods should cross over each other. Then ask the rods to indicate a yes. Once again, the rods should cross. When you ask for the rods to indicate the answer no, they should remain stationary. Now you have your code.

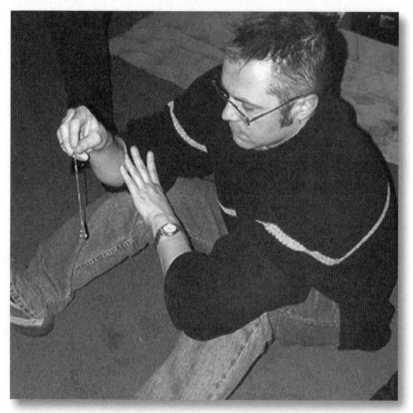

Crystal dowsing at Bowden House

Surprisingly, the process does achieve some remarkable results. I have 'interviewed' alleged entities through this process many times and on almost every occasion, information such as dates, places and names can be historically matched.

So how does it really work? Well, crystal, wood, metal, these are all natural properties of our planet and have been part of the earth for millions of years. We all know that metal is an electrical conductor, so is it reasonable to assume that perhaps metal dowsing rods can actually react to the magnetic forces of Mother Nature? If, as many believe, surviving energy or spirit is a perfectly natural phenomenon of life on earth, then can such instruments, be they metal, wood or crystal, also detect and even communicate with an intelligent form of energy? Or are we all just deluding ourselves? Is it possible that dowsing merely interplays with our own subconscious and creates a scenario that appeals to the ghost hunter? As I mentioned earlier, the paranormal always raises more questions than answers.

Spirit guides

We all go through tough times at certain points in our lives caused mainly by our own human failings, such as mistakes, unwise decisions or, that old devil himself, simple bad luck. Many people learn from their failings and become stronger and wiser, whereas others appear to plod along through life gullibly accepting whatever is thrown at them.

We certainly possess free will, intelligence and intuition, but occasionally in life a problem crops up that has no real solution. Then, religious or not, we find ourselves looking up to the heavens and muttering the immortal words that clergyman love to hear: 'Oh God, please help me!'

Strangely enough, most of the time an answer to the problem appears from the most unexpected source, giving you the feeling that you have been released from the stress at last and subsequently you find yourself believing that your prayers have been answered. Religion states that God is the ultimate guide through which we shape our lives, but what of our own inner self, our psychic ability? Have you ever been faced with a decision and felt the feeling deep inside of you crying out for you to say no? Or the warm glow that indicates that another proposal is indeed the right one for you?

Some in today's peer-led society ignore human instinct, the most basic natural ability we have. I am going to go out on a limb here and say that I firmly believe that it's possible that each and every one of us has a spirit guide. I have come to this conclusion not by research, but by personal experience, and I hold that individual knowledge close to my heart.

Having said that, I do have a theory that goes like this. What if when we die, instead of going forward, some of us are sent back to guide ourselves through the mistakes we made in mortal life, not so much to rectify, but to learn/watch first hand the errors we made. Could it be that the subconscious guardian we sense is, in fact, ourselves?

Ley lines

The human race evolved on this planet. We are all part of the natural world, just as much as the humming bird or the great rain forests. Everything on the planet has a natural order. Our world and all its living creatures all exist within an electromagnetic field. Using detection devices such EMF meters, divining rods and so on, lines of energy can indeed be traced and documented. Not surprisingly, many of these ley lines or energy lines are found on haunted sites.

Ley lines apparently crisscross the planet in ever-increasing patterns. I believe they maintain the balance of the vast levels of energy present in order for our planet to sustain existence. They are like the arteries, and work as an electrical circuit taking energy given out by life forms and then reintroducing it back into the mix.

Ancient humans allegedly found a way to channel these earth energies and even create their own ley lines in order to map vast amounts of land. It all sounds far-fetched but consider this: perhaps humankind once possessed knowledge far beyond our imagining. Before technology, we all lived off the land and were in tune with the planet. With the introduction of new teachings and cultures, maybe this knowledge ceased to be passed down until eventually it was lost and forgotten.

Orbs

These strange anomalies have been the subject of many discussions over the years. Now it is certainly the case that you can get lens flare or reflections from a flash; in fact any light bouncing around the room will reflect in the lens of a digital camera. But these are generally recognised by an experienced investigator or photographer straight away and thus dismissed. As to whether orbs are disincarnate spirits, this is for me a little far-fetched. Even if they were proved to be something unknown appearing beyond our normal visual range, there would still be no definitive proof that they were ghosts.

There was, however, one occasion where a display of lights in an old Tudor mansion pushed the theory of orbs to the limit. Marion had channelled the spirit of a 17th-century young girl and using automatic writing had drawn a picture of an eye, claiming it to be the colour blue. Then in her trance-like state, she proceeded to point eagerly around the room. We had no idea of the meaning of this action other than it could have been an amusing game of charades.

I was pondering on this the next night as I sat in the control room with two of my colleagues going through the digital pictures I had taken earlier that night. Looking through the viewfinder of the camera, there in the corner was a small logo of an eye, exactly the same design as Marion had drawn during the séance. Maybe a game of charades wasn't that ridiculous a notion after all, for the answer appeared plain. She had been trying to say 'Look.' An excited cry from my colleagues broke my thoughts and I gazed in amazement at the monitor screens. Downstairs in the Great Hall, orb after orb appeared flitting and darting around the huge oak dining table.

The atmosphere in the hall that night when I went down to investigate was electric, every hair on my arms stood up and the old cliché of the hairs on the back of the neck now became an understated experience. The lights were being filmed by an infrared mini-cam, but nothing could be seen with the naked eye. However, the display went on for six hours or more before it abruptly stopped.

Some experts say it was dust or seed pollen that somehow managed to find its way into the house, but you have to take into account the fact that our team staked out the building for five days and nights. Realistically at some point dust particles are going to appear, but what are the chances of this happening just once, for a few hours, on one solitary night with all draught areas blocked?

I am not totally convinced even to this day that what we were actually witnessing was indeed disembodied spirits at play, but retaining an open mind I offered my thanks, as it did appear that on this occasion my patience had been rewarded. Whatever the cause, the orb phenomena will continue to be a hot topic of debate for many years to come.

Ghosts

There are many different types of ghosts, the most common being the aptly named replay ghost. This particular apparition is not a lost soul or conscious spirit, but rather a memory trace with visual effects. A typical example is the often heard story of the ghost of the grey lady who walks the stairway or castle walkway on certain nights of the year. The theory is that if at some point in the past a violent or highly charged emotional incident occurred in a place, then somehow the psychokinetic energy of that event is absorbed into the crystalline structure embedded within the very walls of a building and, under the correct electromagnetic environmental conditions, can be replayed like a video player. Since many old castles were built with crystalline properties in the stone, it's hardly surprising that the majority of these replay ghosts are often reported in castles from all around the world.

A haunting

There are many reasons for a haunting. It could be that someone who died just doesn't want to move on, they want to stay at home in surroundings they recognise and trust. Some people die so suddenly that are unaware that they have in fact died. Their consciousness creates the illusion that the world around them is normal so they carry on with their daily routine. There's a perfect example of this in the film *The Others*.

The interactive ghost

This type of ghost is not only self aware and intelligent, but also capable of interacting with us and they can even make themselves visible as what we call a manifestation. Some people claim to have heard a ghost actually speak to them. This is usually a kind of one-to-one telepathic link that would explain why it is very rare that two people can hear the voice at the same time.

From reports I have read and what I have experienced myself, the interactive ghost has tactile capabilities. It can touch you, stroke your hair or face or even poke you in the back to gain your attention. Some even seem capable of manufacturing odours that were associated with them when they were alive, such as tobacco, flowers or perfume.

The ghost hunter's kitbag

Apart from sandwiches, torch, flask of tea and a spare pair of underpants (yes, it can get scary), it really depends on the individual as to the contents of his or her kitbag. Generally you will need: a notepad and pen to jot down times and notes; a digital camera to photograph the haunted areas in the hope of capturing anomalies, such as misty apparitions or orbs; a compass to detect electromagnetic fluctuations; a wristwatch; an audio recording device to record EVPs, either digital or a simple tape recorder; a video or DV camera with night vision, and, if you are feeling really adventurous, a selection of objects such as marbles, walnuts or perhaps an old item belonging to the property that you can use in a controlled object experiment. However, by far the greatest tool is your own common sense. Never attribute anything to ghosts that can be easily explained. To understand the procedures involved in ghost detection fully, I have listed below 10 of the most common occurrences that you may encounter together with a summary of basic field equipment.

1. Cold spots in areas where no draught can be detected.
2. Lights that flicker, electrical equipment malfunctions and battery drainage.
3. Feelings that you are not alone or of being watched.
4. Bangs, scrapes, footsteps and strange odours.
5. A feeling of static electricity emanating through your body.
6. Whispering voices.
7. Emotional changes, including hot and cold flushes.
8. Blue flashes or orbs of light that catch the eye.
9. Shadows seen in your peripheral vision.
10. Objects that mysteriously disappear and then reappear later in a place you would least expect to find.

EMF meters

Although it was never designed for such a practice, the old favourite for locating ghosts is the electromagnetic field (EMF) meter. Roughly about the size of a mobile phone this compact device has been featured in many ghost hunting TV shows over the years. The principle of the EMF meter is that it apparently detects the electromagnetic field given off by ghosts and either bleeps or flashes a red light whenever a ghost is in the vicinity. Unfortunately, very few investigators out there using this apparatus are adequately qualified to recognise what it is they are actually detecting.

Electromagnetic fields have two elements: a magnetic field and an electrical field that are created wherever there is a flow of electricity. A standard EMF meter will register any electrical current within its range. For example a TV set will still register even if it is switched off, if the mains are plugged in and the current is still flowing.

EMF devices will also detect overhead power cables, microwave ovens and mobile phones. This being the case, it is extremely difficult to focus on what is potentially paranormal in a modern-day haunted house, which is why it is vital that you conduct a baseline test around each room before you start, noting down any source of EMF together with humidity and temperature. Any unusual readings registered during your investigation can then be compared with your original baseline readings.

If you hold a compass, you can clearly see that the planet has her own natural magnetic field called the geomagnetic field. It is widely known that our planet produces EMFs in the form of static fields; however, these naturally produced EMFs are low in strength, registering only around 8Hz. Furthermore, we humans also emit an EMF frequency and although ours is of a low scale, certain meters can trick a group of ghost hunters into believing that they are in the company of paranormal visitors. Theoretically, it is generally accepted that ghosts emit a low-frequency EMF field, roughly below the 60Hz indicator ranging in strength between 2.0 and 7.0 mG, standing for milliGauss. A Gauss is a common unit of measurement for the strength of magnetic fields. According to many researchers, the Trifield EMF meter is by far the best suited to detecting ghosts and combines all the features needed for fast, accurate measurements of electromagnetic fields. It independently measures both electric and magnetic fields, and is properly scaled to indicate the full magnitude of currents produced by each type of field inside a conductive body. As a result, it 'sees' much more than any other electromagnetic pollution meter.

Although you will see some investigators wandering around with the meter scanning the immediate area like Spock out of *Star Trek*, it is probably more advisable to place the device in a stationary position in a reputed haunted area and simply wait for it to alert you when it senses an EMF source.

Recording the voices of spirits

The procedure for electronic voice phenomena (EVP) is simple. Set up your tape or digital recording device in an area you believe to be haunted. Ensure that everybody present is aware that you are conducting this experiment and to remain still and quiet for the 10 or so minutes you require. Switch the recorder on and ask for somebody to talk to you, ask them their name, what they do, is this their house and so on. Although you will not hear anything when conducting this experiment, you may find answers to your questions when you play the recording back, but be careful how you perceive any voices found. Some EVPs are not always that straightforward and are surprisingly found when the recording is either speeded up or slowed down.

Another practical method is to set the recorder running and leave the area for a time, ensuring that nobody has access to the location chosen. However, my favourite has to be the 'knock, knock' EVP. Rather than asking for spoken words, demonstrate that you wish them to knock on the floor or wall for you three times... I will leave that one for you to enjoy.

What is EVP?

Voices apparently from the other side are recorded within the static white noise of untuned radios, TV sets and are perceived as spirits delivering messages to the world. It sounds fanciful, but to the 21st-century ghost hunter, EVP is rapidly becoming the most recognised procedure for providing proof of an afterlife.

Before his death in 1931, Thomas Edison had been working on an audio machine that he claimed would prove contact with the spirit world, but it all really began with Friedrich Jurgenson, an archaeologist and philosopher who while out one day recording birdsong with a tape recorder, discovered human voices on the playback, although no one had been anywhere in the vicinity at the time of the recording.

EVP was born and from there many great minds began to research the possibilities of talking to the dead, including the UK pioneer of EVP, Raymond Cass. It wasn't until the late 1970s and early '80s that an apparent working device was unveiled by an American company called Meta Science led by George W. Meek. Called the spiritcom, conversations with the spirit world, some of which lasted up to an hour, were successfully recorded, before suddenly, inexplicably, the device stopped working for good.

Many EVPs are dismissed simply because the recording of a voice is so short and muddled with static it could really be anything. Under these conditions, once again our brain steps in and attempts to find patterns in the noise that ultimately sound like words. Currently, experiments with infrasound, a low-bass frequency inaudible to the human ear, caused by motorway traffic, trains and other low-level vibrations have been found to cause mood swings, depression and even hallucinations in certain individuals. High levels of infrasound are commonly found in the vicinity of haunted houses, indicating that perhaps people really are sensing or seeing ghosts but not in the same way as one might expect.

We all hear at different frequencies. For example, a household pet cat can hear up to 60,000Hz, whereas we humans can only hear on the frequency of just over 20Hz. If ghosts really do exist on a different dimensional level, then this would explain why dogs and cats can apparently sense or even hear spirits operating on frequencies similar to their own. I believe that EVP works and is worthy of further study.

On *Northern Ireland's Greatest Haunts*, I was very fortunate to have Mark Cowden on the team, who proved time and time again to be a valuable asset to the series with his expert knowledge and analysis regarding EVP.

Mark Cowden on EVP

EVP is the ability to record voices of a paranormal origin on to electronic equipment. Methods of recording EVP have advanced to an astounding level over the past decade and now in the 21st century, it's happening all over the world, baffling scientists and experts who are now being forced to rethink many of the theories they thought so long to be true. One of the newest advances that I have personally witnessed with EVP is a new method called frequency scanning. While we were filming *Northern Ireland's Greatest Haunts* at Woburn House for the BBC (see page 164), I decided to try a different approach and monitor our medium Marion Goodfellow while she was asking questions to alleged spirits, rather than just the room. The results were amazing. Every time the medium asked a question, a response registered on my computer. No question, no response. I could actually see on my graphs and monitors that something unknown appeared to be making intelligent contact.

As far as I am aware, this was a first in the paranormal field of research and as such is something that we plan to concentrate on in the near future. Advanced recording methods and sophisticated recording devices are now capable of scanning a wide range of frequencies previously inaccessible to the human ear. This enables paranormal investigators to capture, record and broadcast voices which are believed to be from the unknown.

Sometimes picking up voices that seem to somehow be imbedded in the atmosphere where a traumatic incident occurred can lead to our team receiving direct answers to questions. The concept may sound strange and impossible to some people, but one must remember that photography was once thought to be paranormal. Unsophisticated peoples believed it stole their soul.

The concept of x-ray technology was thought to have paranormal qualities when the idea first came about and it is now being used in every medical centre in the world. Gravity existed before it was discovered and scientifically explained, although the specifics of exactly how it worked would have blown the minds of people living in a non-scientific period.

Throughout the history of mankind, things we couldn't explain have scared us, and have often been labelled as witchcraft. Many of those things are now a part of science and have been introduced into our everyday lives. Many we can't live without. Even today, people fear what they don't understand and can't explain, but this does not mean that it is not possible. This does not mean that it will not someday be explainable. What is paranormal today may be common science tomorrow.

Mark L. Cowden

Knock, knock – who's there?

During an investigation at Tamworth Castle in Staffordshire, investigator John Sutton and I conducted an EVP experiment on the staircase adjacent to the entrance hall. At the time I had my doubts about EVP, simply because the voices picked up on tape recorders can easily be dismissed as nothing but a tape spool noise effect. Psychologically, if you really want to hear a ghostly voice in amongst the white noise, generally you will, but again this is usually a result of the brain attempting to pattern particular noises into something an individual can easily recognise, whereas today with the introduction of digital equipment, the scientific analysis of EVPs has proved to be far more reliable.

On this occasion, to rule out the often inadmissible evidence of voices, I decided to utilise the old Victorian method of table tapping or in this particular case stair rapping. John and I had set up two microphones at either end of the stairway and armed with headphones proceeded to ask the obligatory question, 'Is there anybody there?' Surprisingly, we both heard a soft noise, barely audible that answered, 'Yes.' I then asked the question, 'Can you do this?' and demonstrated my request by knocking twice on the wooden stair. There was a short pause and then two knocks were clearly heard by both of us.

To be sure of ruling out foul play, I asked John to check downstairs to ensure that we were indeed alone and no practical jokers had found their way into the building. No natural source could be found to explain the noises and furthermore no one was present beneath the stairs or in the immediate vicinity. In fact, the remainder of the team were all on the other side of the castle conducting their own experiments.

We had barely settled down to continue when the alleged entity began to knock on the microphones. Astonished, we sat and listened as a series of muffled thumps came through the headphones. I called out that if they were children to knock five times. The muffled knocks ceased abruptly followed by a long pause. Then, five loud knocks came back, clear enough now to be heard without the aid of the headphones. We sat for a further hour trying to cause some more responses, but were met by dead silence. We found no explanation for what we had heard and strangely enough when the tape was replayed the sounds were not recorded.

The paranormal is a minefield of questions and answers that are never resolved, but as you begin to investigate, collect and examine your evidence your thirst for knowledge suddenly evolves into something a little less egotistical. You begin to dwell on what life must have been like for the ghosts of the people you seek, you begin to care rather than fear, your curiosity turns to wonder and when that happens you feel blessed to have touched the past in some small way.

Cold spots

Almost every haunted house has a cold spot. In fact, some boast many in various rooms or hallways. The unique, soft, velvety touch of a cool draught as an entity passes you by is unmistakable once felt for the first time. The energy of a ghost is said to cause the drop in temperature and this is easily checked by your baseline test. If when you arrived you jotted down that an area in one particular room felt unusually cold and remains so throughout your visit then there is often a plausible explanation, such as a natural draught emanating through floorboards, cracks in the ceiling or windows that is easily checked with the use of a duck feather (another cheap piece of kit).

Ghosts are people

It's a common misconception that all ghosts are dark, evil entities dripping in ectoplasm intent on doing bad deeds. They are not. Most are benign and completely harmless. That isn't to say that you should stumble around investigating hauntings believing you are untouchable, for there are rare documented cases where extreme poltergeist activity can cause actual bodily harm, mainly from objects hurling themselves through the air. However, in all my years studying these phenomenon, I have ever only witnessed what appeared to be the work of a poltergeist twice and on both occasions there was no intent to harm.

In reality, the only assailant you have to be wary of is yourself and your own fear of the unknown, for when faced with an apparent paranormal situation your imagination often works against you rather than for you, and under those conditions panic can lead to unnecessary accidents.

Ghosts are people. They once had a physical life as we do now and should therefore be treated with an equal level of respect, which is why I prefer to observe rather than hunt. The term 'ghost hunter' is a generalist title that I am not fond of, for to hunt something you have to adopt a predatory stance and in doing so your adversary will often simply retreat or hide away. Television programmes that feature celebrities attempting to force spirits out to play up for the cameras by questioning their bravery and even hurling insults are to be ignored by anybody seriously studying these phenomena.

In the lower catacombs at the Tower of London

Another myth is that you have to be in darkness to encounter a ghost. Well, the fact is that you don't. Hollywood films are mainly to blame for this and in any case sitting in the dark only ignites your imagination. Light depravation is the main culprit for over 40% of ghost sightings and I have lost count of the number of accidents caused by people shuffling around a location with no lighting.

There is a great divide between so-called reality entertainment and serious paranormal investigation, and running around in the dark screaming at the slightest noise is not a good example of how paranormal investigations are conducted. I suggest a more relaxed approach, such as soft lighting, playing classical music, introducing ornaments or toys: anything, in fact, that the ghostly inhabitant would recognise from his or her lifetime. This will achieve an immediate sense of understanding between yourself and whoever is there. It is advisable to try and keep your team numbers down to a minimum of four, six at the most, depending on the size of the building and to avoid invading the building all at once. Go in alone, walk around, introduce yourself, tell them why you are here, that you mean them no harm and make it perfectly clear that you understand if they have no wish to make themselves known to you.

It takes time and sounds rather silly to follow these procedures when standing in an empty room or corridor of a reputed haunted house, but with patience, respect and a little luck you may just be pleasantly surprised.

Above all, enjoy your experiences and keep safe.

Index